SECRETS OF BREAKING INTO THE FILM AND TV BUSINESS

SECRETS OF BREAKING INTO THE FILM AND TV BUSINESS

TOOLS AND TRICKS FOR TODAY'S DIRECTORS, WRITERS, AND ACTORS

DEAN SILVERS

wm

WILLIAM MORROW
An Imprint of HarperCollinsPublishers

HarperCollins books may be purchased for educational, business, or sales promotional use. For information please e-mail the Special Markets Department at SPsales@harpercollins.com.

FIRST EDITION

Designed by Diahann Sturge

Library of Congress Cataloging-in-Publication Data has been applied for.

ISBN 978-0-06-228006-0

14 15 16 17 18 OV/RRD 10 9 8 7 6 5 4 3 2 1

Dedicated to
Marlen,
and to Forrest and Tyler

CONTENTS

OBSTACLES TO ENTERING THE INDUSTRY—AND HOW TO GET AROUND THEM

Everything You Thought You Knew About the
Film and Television Industry? . . . Fuhgeddaboudit!

I've made films. I'm making films, not only as a filmmaker, but as a deal maker, marketer, entertainment lawyer, producer, facilitator, distributor, talent evaluator, and more.

I know what it's like to be a beginner. To have questions. And to feel uncertain of the right moves to make on pressure-packed movie sets where minutes can mean thousands or millions of dollars. That's why this book is different. Working closely with major talent and creative minds—taking abstract ideas and story threads and turning them into movies—has exposed me to perspectives, concepts, and inventions of thought that you can't really fathom unless you've been in those trenches.

People love film. We've all got our favorite movie moments. Iconic scenes that linger in the memory long after the details of the plot and character fade: Natalie Portman's final dance in *Black Swan*, the title fight in *Raging Bull*, Steve Carell's chest waxing in *The 40-Year-Old Virgin*, Jessica Chastain's look at a dead Osama bin Laden in *Zero Dark Thirty*, the final lift in *Dirty Dancing*, E.T. flying a bike against a moon backdrop in *E.T.*, the way Humphrey Bogart says good-bye to Ingrid Bergman in *Casablanca*—powerful, astonishing sequences that thrill us, move us, and inspire us.

And let us not forget that we are also in a golden age of superb cinematic television. Whether it be *Breaking Bad, Mad Men, Homeland, The Office,* or *Game of Thrones,* we are witnessing the sort of high-quality television that we have not seen in years, if ever.

The gravitational pull of such doesn't only spawn celebrity Twitter followers and fawning fan blogs—remember, the film and television industry is also an engine of enormous economic horsepower. Over time America has become a nation that imports more goods than it exports—yet the film and television industry is probably our greatest export, so succeeding in this industry can only strengthen our economy. Even in a slow economy, the film and television industry is a soaring American success story, and it continues to experience explosive growth.

It's no wonder everyone wants to be in the film and television industry. There are legions of aspiring filmmakers, but the mechanisms for entry, the rules for how to play the game and win, have never been sequentially laid out before—not in other books, nor in lectures, not even in the most respected film schools and academies. In short: No one is telling you how to make a strong film, be seen by the right people, and make a career.

But I am.

What was I thinking?
*   It's July 8, in the middle of a hot summer. My wife and kids have long since gone to sleep, but I'm pacing*

the floors of my New York City apartment. It's about 3:45 ... a.m. It's late—very late. Or rather very early ...

I'm about to start the first day of shooting a feature film. I'm the sole producer. And I'm rehashing the disastrous position I've gotten myself into. You see, until now, I'd spent most of my life nowhere near the film industry. I was actually going to be part of a real-life movie set. I was going to be a producer—I even signed my name on the dotted line. The last time I signed my name on a dotted line for a movie was when I signed up for my Blockbuster Rewards card (which was laminated, so I knew at least someone in the "biz" appreciated my movie taste, even if Blockbuster is now a defunct video chain store). I'm a former religious studies | comparative literature major (and let me tell you, there aren't a whole lot of jobs in that field). I've got a PhD, a law degree, and a master's degree. But I have never been on the set of a feature film. And yet, come sunrise, that's where I'll be, as the sole producer of a full-length, narrative feature film.

The writer and director—the person everything hinges on—has never written or directed a feature film before. He's a copywriter for a public relations organization. In his midthirties, he's ancient for the industry and antediluvian for someone just starting his feature-film career. He's made a couple of shorts, but he doesn't even know the things he doesn't know about making full-length movies.

I have a ridiculously small budget of $75,000, and we're shooting with donated, expensive 35-millimeter film—the kind they use for big Hollywood movies. Everyone is working for free, we're begging equipment houses to let us borrow what we need for the shoot, and *my line producer (who runs the logistics of the entire production) abruptly left the project one day ago.*

If I had the slightest connection to anyone in the film business, I would have known this script had been passed on by everyone. For years. It's a dark comedy about incest. A dead project. Unmakable. I have no mentor, no guide, no one to call if things go south. But I saw some real potential in what the script could be.

And that's how I started my career in film.

The film was Spanking the Monkey, *and, fortunately for me, those early-hour voices of doom were entirely wrong.* Spanking *went on to be a significant success, winning the Audience Award at Sundance, garnering career-making reviews, gaining theatrical distribution through Fine Line Features, and selling well overseas. The neophyte director was David O. Russell, who would go on to have some impressive hits with films like* Flirting with Disaster, Three Kings, The Fighter, Silver Linings Playbook, *and* American Hustle.

The story of that achievement is really the launching point for this book: How did I get myself in a position to produce a film? And once I got there, how did I actually make a career in this wonderful, crazy industry? And how can first-time directors, actors, and writers make a career?

I did plenty of heavy lifting on that film (and others)—literally: pulling cable, hoisting camera dollies, and driving equipment trucks. That's how it started. With *Spanking*, I was lucky I didn't really know the conventional wisdom about breaking into film because if I had, I would have failed—quickly and probably spectacularly. What we were trying to do was so off-the-map nuts, I had to think in counterintuitive ways just to keep the entire thing from running off the rails. I had to break rules. I had to invent my own way of operating. Clichés are awful in screenplays, but they often capture enduring truths. And on my first film, while I discovered that "ignorance truly is bliss," I also discovered a great pathway to some invaluable knowledge.

What I've gleaned here are the things I've learned by struggling, failing, fighting, pulling rabbits out of hats (and other places), and figuring out how to make things happen the way I needed them to. Here you'll find strategies from the front lines—ideas you'll never be taught in any film school or lectures, concepts that are time-tested and successful.

Not many people have taken the path I have taken, and a part of my success has been an understanding that while there are no immutable laws in the film and television industry, there are reliable truths that have formed my own personal credo, and which comprise the foundation for the ideas in this book.

I wanted to write this book because I was really angry. Howard Beale in *Network* mad. Today so many people are being misled and taken advantage of; they are given bad advice or models that are totally outdated, ineffective, costly, exploitative . . . and sometimes just outright embarrassing.

I'm also distressed that these same people say it's impossible to succeed in the media industry without a diploma from one of the two or three elite film schools, or any film school for that matter, or without the right connections. It's wrong. All of it. Unequivocally. So I decided to write this book to set the record straight, to truly help people pursue their dreams.

This book is for anyone and everyone with a creative spark and the ambition to work in the film and television industry. The path to success winds a different route than it used to. You just have to pay attention to a new set of directions to navigate the way.

In this book I am focusing on making films, but be aware that the skills you need to succeed in the film and television industries are quickly becoming interchangeable. When you succeed with your film or your short using the lessons in this book, you will have great career opportunities in both the film and television industries.

The Traditional Model

The traditional model was to have your film accepted into a prestigious film festival, or you would go to an elite film school, get an education, and be successful in the film industry. Elite film schools were perhaps once worth the investment. But this is no longer the case. The sales pitch that these schools, festivals, and workshops traditionally used—and still exploit today—focuses on three things:

1. Film theory and research
2. Training on complex, professional film equipment
3. Industry contacts to increase your chances of getting into the business

Thanks to the Internet, the film "theory" they teach in film classes is available everywhere. Now, truly anyone can get free or relatively inexpensive online film lectures from MIT, UCLA, or any number of hallowed institutions of higher learning. You can give yourself the equivalent of a master of arts in film simply by searching online. There are blogs, groups, entire sites devoted to film theory and film craft. See a movie, then go to RottenTomatoes.com and read reviews from respectable film critics; why learn film theory on just old movies when you can learn from prominent critics of today's cinema? You can do it all yourself.

Equipment is now cheap and easy to use. Anyone can buy or rent a simple camera and editing software, learn to use them from YouTube videos, forums, online classes, and then bang—you can make a film. Most of your postproduction needs can fit on a laptop. You don't need semesters of classes to figure out what you're doing technically; you need a few days. Learning is now only as far away as a click on your computer.

And as far as jobs and industry contacts . . . I can't tell you how many frustrated filmmakers I meet who have graduated and used their school's "connections" to land them, at best, a modest job as an assistant editor on a cable TV show, or a job as an electrician in the independent film world. They all have the same complaint. It's not how their dream was supposed to turn out. They're looking for a way to make it in the movies—as a writer, director, actor, producer, editor—not someone who simply makes ends meet.

But what's more important is the gaping hole between what they teach you in many film schools and what they *don't* teach you. They don't teach you how to create for the marketplace, how to sell a film, and how to foster a career. Making a film isn't like any other vocation. If you can make the grade in medical school, you graduate, become a resident, and pretty soon you'll become a doctor. Same goes for law school, nursing school, trade schools—but not for film schools.

Same thing with the film festival route. For example, the 1990s saw many films come out of nowhere and get into the Sundance Film Festival. Many were then acquired by a distributor, and a career was launched (think Steven Soderbergh,

Quentin Tarantino, David O. Russell, Kevin Smith). This still happens, but with new-media technology allowing many, many more films to be made, approximately twelve-thousand-plus films are submitted for fewer than two hundred positions. Even if you like your odds, you may as well be buying a lottery ticket.

The New Model

> ### The Three Building Blocks
>
> 1. The Internet—Film Theory and Research
> 2. New-Media Technology—Equipment
> 3. The New Social-Media Environment—
>   Marketing and Distribution

I have created a new model—the Three Building Blocks—which will help you become successful in the entertainment industry. These tenets are based upon my experience, and reflect three major changes in the media environment that you can use in order to make it in the film and television industry.

The Internet—Film Theory and Research

We live in a very busy, media-savvy society, where tomorrow's news becomes yesterday's story very quickly. Everything happens at Internet speed now—fast news cycles, short attention spans, and shorter cultural memory. The Internet has really changed everything. . . . And I mean *everything*. The Internet is unlike any medium before it. You often hear this, but take a moment to realize that the Internet is actually comprised of all media that came before it—it has visual, audio, interactive, text, and telephone capabilities . . . all in one.

How did we do anything before the Internet? What now takes thirty minutes would have taken hours before. The way we write, read, shop, digest entertainment, research, get our news, have relationships—they have all undergone an absolute revolution. You can now learn everything they teach in film school in the comfort of your own home. Want to learn about Alfred Hitchcock? Take a course . . . online. Want to know about the French New Wave? Google it. Want to study Quentin Tarantino? Judd Apatow? Look up the only film Charles Laughton was credited as a director? It's a click away.

New-Media Technology—Equipment

Today, if you've got a cell-phone camera you can be a filmmaker. You can hold an entire postproduction house in your lap. The cost of equipment has decreased radically in these last few years, and the sophistication of modern equipment has made it much easier to learn how to use. You used to need a postproduction house, an audio-mixing room, editorial suites, loop groups, colorists, and artists. Now you don't. Everything has changed. Making moving pictures has finally become democratic: Anyone can make a movie. The beauty of Building Block Two is not only that the new technological equipment is relatively inexpensive to acquire, but it no longer takes years of apprenticeship to learn how to use. Motivated individuals in this field are often able to achieve competence and expertise quickly. Consequently, there are more people with special-effects talents and multiple skills than ever before, thus making the labor pool much more accessible to you on your future projects.

Of course making a *good movie* is a totally different story, but this book will give you the tools for doing just that.

The New Social-Media Environment—Marketing and Distribution

Even if making a film is easier, selling it is harder. Marketing and promotion are more difficult. Because it is so easy to make films, many more are being made, so getting your film seen and discovered is now much harder. Building a career has become more inscrutable, confusing, and complex. We are also experiencing a cultural explosion in our new social-media environment, a transformation as revolutionary as the Internet was. But lecturers, bloggers, or film academies don't focus enough on this revolution overtaking the industry. The decentralization of services and the proliferation of technology for marketing and distribution are virtually changing the ground under our feet.

You used to need teams of people to distribute and promote your film. Now you don't. And knowing and mastering the new social-media environment are keys to creating your own success in the media industry. I will show you how to create, distribute, and promote something that will be seen by those who can help you achieve your career goals.

And nowadays there are many new and expanding outlets eager for new product. The onset of the new digital-distribution revolution has vastly expanded markets. So-called experts point to the music industry as an example of the shrinking of an industry due to digital decentralization (i.e., how easy and inexpensive it is now to distribute and have access to music), but they have it backwards. Sure, the top echelon of the music industry has been decimated, but now more musicians than ever are making music, being heard and seen, and from this initial exposure, making a career through ancillary markets like touring and merchandising. Just look what YouTube has become.

Moreover, new venues for film have exploded onto the marketplace, and the industry's thirst for new talent has never been this significant. Consider this: The US film and television business is probably the healthiest in our country today, and in the international marketplace as well. Its workers have on average the highest annual salaries (sports figures are number two, followed by Wall Street). For its part, the film and television distribution industry is also phenomenally good at what it does and is continually and aggressively seeking new films, talent, and product.

So that little idea you have for a movie isn't just the currency of a filmmaking dream; it's the driver of one of the most powerful economic engines in the world. Anyone who is working in this industry today is going to be curious to see what you've got.

The traditional models no longer work, but using my Three Building Blocks will help you make what the film and television industry cannot live without—a good, original, and highly marketable product.

The Road Map: How to Apply the Three Building Blocks to Your Career

Using my Three Building Blocks will help you create your career in the entertainment industry through a specific process:

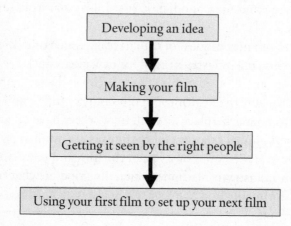

Each of these steps will be broken down in this book. We will look at the *entire* process, covering creative issues, logistics, legal paperwork and considerations, practical advice, and more.

I go through specific case studies—real films, real war stories, real problems, and real solutions. We will go through the whole process of making a movie, from the blinking cursor at the top of your first blank screenplay page all the way to the final credit roll in your neighborhood multiplex.

At every step we'll employ an interactive process by:

- setting the context and stakes through real-life stories;
- presenting a dilemma and challenging you to consider solutions;

- explaining how we solved a creative, logistical, or business problem; and
- applying these situations to your own process of creating, shooting, editing, marketing, promoting, and selling your work.

In every instance you'll learn from my mistakes, my escapes from disaster, and my triumphs. It's how to stop talking about making movies and how to start actually doing it—reflected through my actual experiences in making movies over the years.

Running Your Own Race

You don't need to know someone to get into the film industry. I didn't know anyone. I started from the ground up and met people and networked. I'm still doing it. A big part of maintaining success and opening up opportunities is building a network of people who can offer support and resources.

"No" doesn't always mean "no." Don't ever take no for an answer. You've heard this advice before, but I include it because it took me years to really understand what it meant. Everyone told me I couldn't be a producer. Or a writer. Or a director. Or a foreign-sales agent. With no exception, everything I've done—at every step—I was always told I couldn't do. And you'll be told the same thing.

But not taking no for an answer doesn't necessarily mean trying the same thing over and over without variation. If you get five passes on your script, submitting it to fifty more production companies doesn't show determination; it shows a lack of imagination. A no is an invitation to solve a problem. Those five passes happened for a reason. If the feedback is always the same, it may mean you need to fix your script. The time to pound the pavement and resubmit your work happens after you've rewritten it. Steve Martin said it best: "Be so good they can't ignore you."

You don't have to sell your soul to succeed. The film industry is a rough business with more than its share of liars and cheaters. But it doesn't have to be that way. You don't have to lie, you don't have to cheat, and you can deal with everyone in an honest way.

Remember, this is your own journey—your own personal race. In an odd way, you are not in competition with anyone else. While it's true that there is a market in the film industry with real competition, at some level the market is irrelevant. Because in a very real way it's no longer about winning the approval of industry gatekeepers and decision makers. The beauty of the digital revolution is that getting into the film industry is as much about exposure and eyeballs as it is about anything else. Every film made can now get some kind of distribution. So success is no longer measured only by getting into a prestigious film festival, winning a limited number of spots at a studio, or getting a high-profile distribution deal. There are many, many mediocre films that can make a splash now and advance the careers of filmmakers simply because of how they're distributed and marketed. That success is not in any way limited by other films crowding the market; it's limited by how creative and resourceful one can be in getting the work out there.

It can be tough remembering this with the media constantly bombarding you with the triumphs of others who are younger, smarter, funnier, and (add your own trait here) than you. But avoid this trap, as it will only frustrate you and distract you from your goals.

The number one concern of people who take my seminar isn't whether or not they have the talent or connections to succeed, it's if they can make it in an industry that's known for "issues of integrity." And the most common reaction I get after a seminar is the relief from realizing that you don't have to sell your soul to make it. And while I acknowledge that's anecdotal evidence, it still is a salient point for filmmakers to understand, and when building your network, you will see how it's possible to surround yourself with good people who can help guide you.

This book will become your official manual, sidekick, guardian angel, and friend for your film and television career. Keep it in your bedroom, dorm room, on set, in your edit, sound, or casting room, or wherever your film is being made. It will help you immensely, particularly when you feel moments of uncertainty or insecurity. When you have a problem, instead of wasting hours worrying about it, just refer to this book.

Now you're ready to begin.

Good luck, have fun, and always enjoy the journey.

DEVELOPMENT: FINDING AN IDEA AND BRINGING IT TO FRUITION

Or, How I Gave Harvey Weinstein the Finger

I'm sitting in the reception area of Miramax's New York offices about to meet with Harvey Weinstein. I'm nervous. I've got butterflies bouncing around the walls of my belly. It's a swarm. My thoughts are bouncing too—will he like my next project? Will he buy it? Will he chew my head off?

The success of my pitch hinges on me being relaxed. And cool. And confident. Which makes me more nervous. I'm about to pitch the concept for Lisa Krueger's second film. She had great success with her first, Manny & Lo. We won the Gotham Open Palm Award, were nominated for four Independent Spirit Awards, and were a festival darling. And Harvey liked the director's next script, a script I was producing with Marlen Hecht.

As the producer, I've now got real industry cachet.

> *And Harvey has already become a larger-than-life figure. He is brilliant. Incredibly successful. Brutal. A great heart. Volatile. A genius, but tough...really tough.*
>
> *The receptionist calls my name. Harvey is ready to see me.*

Let's back up for a moment. Before you can sell a script, you have to own or write one, and before you can do that, significant creative work needs to be done. The process that gets you to that final script—coming up with an idea, writing (or optioning), and then having it rewritten over and over (and over) as you and your team cut, improve, shape, rethink, and perfect it—is called development.

What Ideas Are Worth Developing?

How often does someone tell you an amusing story or anecdote and follow it by saying, "Wouldn't that make a great movie?" We've all heard it now and then, and in my line of work, I hear it far more often than I need to. Most of the time, what people think will make a great movie rarely does. Making great movies is more about capturing a *theory* of reality, a story that feels true to life but is bigger, deeper, with transcendent highs and poignant lows. If films are simply direct copies of real life, they are documentaries. Documentaries can be great dramatic films, but that's an entirely different thing.

Films have to move us. People don't want to *think* when they see a movie; they want to *feel*. Ever wonder why Bruce Willis has to save the world *and* save his wife or daughter in all those action movies? Because that's where the emotion is. There's an old development saying that goes, "Develop what you know."

And while that's true, it's only half the story. Develop what you know, but don't be afraid (after a lot of research) to create what you don't know, a strategy that helps enormously when you are trying to create unusual and interesting ideas. But most important, you also have to develop what you love. Something you feel passionate about, something that inspires you.

Market Rules

This is where things get a little muddy. Although it's crucial to develop and/or write something you feel passionate about, if that passion is a dark, depressing vision of a dysfunctional family, no one is going to want to fund or buy it, which means no one is going to see it. You're trying to carve out a career in show *business*, not in show *art*. And like it or not, that business is run by commerce, not just creativity.

In today's media world, you're not just competing against the thousands of other movies made every year. You're trying to get someone to leave their comfortable couch and turn away from their laptops, Internet, video games, Netflix, and thousands of TV channels. On top of that, you're asking them to reach into their pocket and pay ten or twelve dollars or sometimes even more to see your movie. So whatever you're putting out there needs to be something off the charts. Something unique. Something that finds a way to distinguish itself from all the other media noise.

It's not easy. Every week the papers are filled with terrific reviews of movies that are smart, well made, passionate projects that no one sees. They close in a week. And the trajectory of a career can go from up to down just like that. I'm not arguing *against* making art, but *for* making art that is commercially viable to an end viewer. If you can do that, the industry will be eating out of the palm of your hand.

At the same time, you shouldn't just chase the market. I was told recently that one of the major writing workshops has been advising its participants (who pay hundreds and hundreds of dollars to attend) to write big-budgeted fantasy films because that's what the industry wants most. To think this would guarantee you sell your script, competing against the 115,000-plus screenplays copywritten every year in the United States alone (many by more seasoned, successful, and "connected" writers), is just plain crazy. Make sure to develop or write what you love, no matter how big or small, but also make sure that it has real market potential. That's going to be an invaluable engine of creativity for you.

You do not have to be a writer. And most important, if writing is not your inclination (i.e., you are an actor, director, or producer), you do not have to write the movie to make a movie. You can develop ideas, and then work with people who will write them for/with you, or option other people's work as well. But don't force ideas. You have to observe, listen, and make sure to write down *all* your ideas (or keep them in a personal e-mail thread or in Word documents). Even looking over bad ideas can eventually lead you to good ones, and those ideas could one day be the makings of a great movie.

Now that we know what we want—inspiration and ideas—where do we find it?

The Internet Is Your Second Brain

Remember the first of my Three Building Blocks—the Internet.

Looking for Inspiration in All the Right Places

If you're having trouble finding something to inspire you to develop or write, there are endless places that will assist you. Go online. There are many screenwriting blogs and websites where you can see loglines, pitches, and synopses. It'll absolutely help you navigate your thinking in the right direction.

One interesting thing to do to inspire you, particularly if you're going to develop and/or write a short or feature film, is to go online to start your search for the student films and first shorts of prominent filmmakers. Take a look at Martin Scorsese's student films, the first shorts of Darren Aronofsky and Jason Reitman, or Martin Brest's first short. It's amazing to see how, in the span of a few minutes, and with no budget, some of our future film virtuosos could create something unique. Something moving. Something you can't stop watching. And it's interesting to see how many shorts they did before they found their own style.

That kind of perspective—how someone with no connections and limited resources was able to find a story that had never been told before—often helps unlock your own creative inspiration.

There are also great books on creativity and process that can inspire you—books by industry icons Sidney Lumet and William Goldman can motivate just about anyone. And look outside the film and television industry—ballet, the sciences, etc. Creativity is creativity. For example, the physicist Richard Feynman has written wonderful articles and books on creativity.

Looking for Ideas in All the Right Places

Now that you're inspired, where do you find your ideas? First, when you're looking for ideas for a film, you have to step outside the hermetically sealed world of cinema. I've seen many film school students and filmmakers who simply watch movie after movie. That kind of insular view of the world shows up in their work. It causes them to make their work derivative. You can spot the scenes in their films that they're aping from other movies. You have to expose yourself to different mediums; read books, for example, that have nothing to do with your movie. Remember: Thousands of wonderful short stories are out there, begging to be turned into short or full-length films. And their authors are often easily approachable—and want to see their work put on the screen. Read as many short stories as you can—the prizewinners, the non-prizewinners. Read the prominent public-domain stories.

Some of your greatest creative inventions will come when your mind is relaxed or occupied with something that has nothing to do with your screenplay. I'm reminded of the story of the great Greek inventor Archimedes, who yelled "Eureka!" when he came up with one of his most famous discoveries regarding water displacement while he was taking a bath. You hear all the time of people being hit with inspiration in the shower, or while they're jogging, or just about to drift off to sleep. Eventually, your idea will come; possibly when you least expect it.

And to give you an advantage, later in this chapter I will tell you the two specific genres to work in that will give you a distinct leg up over your fellow filmmakers.

"Hit Single" Theory of Success

Years ago, one of the most successful agents I have ever met (he was at William Morris at the time) said something that has stayed with me for years. He called it his "Hit Single" theory. According to him, all creative industries want something new. In fact they're desperate for it. However, the idea (at least for your first film) can't be so new that it feels untested and disconnected from conventional popular taste. Successful artists, he said, always blend something new and something old in their initial works. The something "old" is subconsciously comforting, while the something "new" is what distinguishes them—whether it be Lady Gaga (Madonna), Jimmy Kimmel (Johnny Carson), *X Factor* (*American Idol*) . . . the list goes on and on.

A specific example, as cited in Charles Duhigg's *The Power of Habit: Why We Do What We Do in Life and Business,* is when Atlanta hip-hop group Outkast released "Hey Ya!" in 2003. They found out that their work, although wonderfully reviewed, was deemed too "new" and did not gain them the audience they had hoped to get.

Arista, their record company, couldn't and didn't want to change their work, so they did the next best thing, following the "hit single" theory. They persuaded radio stations nationwide to play Outkast's new song sandwiched in between two non-Outkast, well-known, familiar songs. In this fashion the listeners "familiarized" themselves with something different.

Along similar lines, scientific studies by professors Robert Zatorre and Valorie Salimpoor from McGill University and the Rotman Research Institute, respectively, show us that dopamine (the hormone that induces the pleasure response) is released in the brain not when successful music rises to its peak in the song, but usually several seconds before, when the brain remembers partial similarities to this new song it's listening to.

They argue that this is the case because, "When we listen to music, these brain networks actually create expectations based on our stored knowledge. . . . Performers intuitively understand this: They manipulate these predictive mechanisms to give us what we want—or to surprise us, perhaps even with something better."

The hit single theory works in all media. I am not saying that you should try to sandwich your film between two successful, familiar films, but rather that when looking for ideas and stories, you should look for something that is familiar, yet takes risks within that familiarity. Quentin Tarantino and Kathryn Bigelow are two examples of prominent of filmmakers taking this approach in their storytelling.

You'll be amazed by what material is available, and by the potential collaborators you will find. Before I had ever produced a film, I was approached by someone who had researched a remarkable true-life story. It was a period piece set in 1960s segregationist Alabama about a great college football player who was also the son of Alabama's pro-civil-rights attorney general. The segregationists in Alabama made life miserable for the boy and his father (who were white), and actually trumped up charges against the attorney general. The boy retaliated—in part—by turning down the chance to go to the University of Alabama (the biggest football power in the country) and choosing the school's rival, Tennessee, instead. The film climaxes with the boy singlehandedly leading Tennessee over Alabama in the Rose Bowl.

Great story. Simple, clean, and with a good message. I wanted to make this movie but had no contacts in the industry. At this stage of my life I had yet to produce, write, or direct a film, but my partner and I wrote an outline, a treatment as to how we saw this story would develop as a film. And then with treatment in hand, the next step was to find a writer. I wanted someone who had a Southern sensibility—if possible, someone old enough to have seen separate bathrooms and restaurant signs that said "Whites Only." I didn't think the story would come to life without someone who had experienced this first-hand. My partner simply looked up a writer from the South whose books were very visual, and whose work we both had read and admired. Then we called him—cold. I had nothing to lose. My partner pitched him the idea and—believe it or not—he loved it. Pat wrote the screenplay, and I sold it as a TV movie to CBS. The film was called *Unconquered,* was very successful, and was nominated for an Emmy.

Now, it helped that "Pat" was the famous novelist Pat Conroy, who already had a successful career with books like *The Great Santini.* Pat of course would go on to write major best sellers, including *The Prince of Tides* (he also wrote the screenplay), which became an Oscar-nominated film directed by, produced by, and starring Barbra Streisand.

But the real lesson here is that you have to try everything. If Pat Conroy had said no, I would have moved on to some-one else. If my second choice had passed, I would have found another. I would have kept trying until I found the right col-laborator, or rewritten my pitch in order to attract the right collaborator until I reached my goal. In addition to novels and nonfiction books, short stories, newspaper and maga-zine articles, blogs, and podcasts, you can always look for off-Broadway theater and well-reviewed small plays, and ap-proach the playwright about optioning his or her play for a film. Did you know that the movie *Casablanca* originally started out as an unpublished stage play entitled *Everybody Comes to Rick's*?!

Your search should have no bounds . . . because you have nothing to lose. If Pat Conroy said yes to my partner and me before I had ever produced anything, there's no telling who will sign on to your project. The stories are out there. It just takes some legwork.

You're now ready to take the next step.

Before you start writing, be aware that currently there are two specific genres that will give you an advantage over the competition.

All Genres Are Not Created Equal—Comedies

Obviously, by definition each genre is not like another, but two specific genres stand out in terms of maximizing your chances for success in the film and television industry as you begin.

Initially it is much easier to separate yourself from the pack with a good comedy. That's certainly worked for me as a producer for *Spanking the Monkey, Manny & Lo,* and *Flirting with Disaster.* And I'm not the only one. Kevin Smith broke in with *Clerks,* Eddie Burns with *The Brothers McMullen,* Richard Linklater with *Slacker,* and Jared Hess with *Napoleon Dynamite.*

All those films have a few things in common: They were inexpensive to make, they were smart, and most became hits without the attachment of big-name talent. That's part of the beauty of comedy: You don't have to hire a huge star. With these kinds of small, intelligent comedies, people come to see the humor, not the celebrities. It didn't matter, for example, who was in *My Big Fat Greek Wedding,* or *Napoleon Dynamite,* or *(500) Days of Summer*; what mattered—and what made them breakout successes—was that they made people laugh.

These kinds of comedies also work because they capture a poignancy about the human condition. Smart humor is always going to do more for your career than gross-out humor, over-the-top sketch humor, spoof humor, and bodily fluid gags. Even in a comedy, people want a movie to move them.

Look at the success of Judd Apatow for inspiration. *Knocked Up*—a frumpy, loser-type guy sleeps with a beautiful woman and must rise to the responsibilities of her pregnancy. *Superbad*—two best friends, in their last days of high school, try to bring alcohol to a party to impress their dream girls. Each movie is funny, wise, energetic, and rich with emotional themes—friendship, maturity, parenthood. We're invited to wonder if Seth Rogen, despite who he is, can become a man. Or whether Jonah Hill and Michael Cera's friendship can survive the different trajectories of their post-high-school lives. Even if you take away the humor, the story stands on its own. The emotional narrative has to draw us in. We want to see what happens next.

But when I say comedy, I mean comedy within the context of an entire story. Create your story, and then make it funny. Don't have a really funny joke or idea, and then make your story around it. I see that all the time, and it is not filmmaking, but rather an expensive "one trick, joke-telling pony." Do not make the mistake of emulating the comedy shorts that are proliferating all over sites like Funny or Die that are just shtick. They may be funny, but they are not storytelling, and will not guarantee a career in the film and television industry.

I have been approached many times by filmmakers who scored extremely high on various comic websites years ago, and do not understand why they still do not have a career in the industry. Because those "joke films" are the cinematic equivalent of empty calories and teach you nothing about structure and building dramatic and comic moments. Don't only tell a joke; tell a story.

And your film doesn't have to be a pure comedy or a complete laugh-fest. It can be science fiction with funny and interesting characters, or even a mystery with funny and light-hearted elements.

I have worked with Stephen Chbosky, whose first film, *The Four Corners of Nowhere,* which he wrote and directed years ago, was a rough but unique mix of comedy and drama. He used the success of that film to create and write the television series *Jericho,* and most recently he wrote and directed *The Perks of Being a Wallflower,* a very powerful blend of comedy and drama.

When you make dramatic films without humor, you get washed in with the rest of those dramatic films, and the opportunity to truly distinguish your work is lost.

All Genres Are Not Created Equal: Sci-Fi

Science fiction is also a good choice for a first short or film. With sci-fi, you can do anything with your story. Literally. Time can go backwards. People can move things with their minds. You can fall in love with an android. And because the nature of the world you create is untethered from the brick-and-mortar reality we normally inhabit, you can alter the traditional norms of storytelling to create something relentlessly original.

In *Looper,* a man comes from the future to face his younger self. In the low-budget film *Moon,* a man struggles with the discovery that his memories have been implanted in him, and that he may be a clone. Films like this rearrange constructive reality, bending the rules of the world in a way that sets up a new arsenal of storytelling elements and variables.

It's smart to look for stories that focus on characters who have to make hard choices, because these invite us to identify with the character. We wonder what we would do in the same situation. Sci-fi allows the filmmaker to jigger with conventional story dilemmas, play with them a bit—or just take a sledgehammer to them. You can tell stories where it's no longer a choice between this girl or that girl, or do I play in the big game or sit out. Is it all right to use my telekinetic power to destroy a rival? Can I trust a robot programmed to work against me? The advantage of the genre is that your story can be truly different because it's a view of the world no one has seen before.

And you'll be able to pay for those computer generated images (CGI) effects because new technologies have made them more affordable. On a recent film we produced we had eighteen big visual special-effects shots. We couldn't find a price we could afford in America, so we Skyped the most prominent visual special-effects company in Serbia and asked for a competitive bid. It didn't take long to discover that the price for our CGI work wasn't just competitive; it was amazing. And so were they.

Now you may think that for your low- or no-budget short you cannot afford special effects, but that is not true. In this industry people take on projects for hundreds of different reasons—it is not always about the money. I have found very high-profile personnel in the special-effects-commercials industry who were willing to work for no money to cross over into films and television. It is your job to do the hard work to find those people who believe you and are willing to take a risk with you on your project. It is hard work, but it *definitely* pays off in the final product.

But you don't have to go to Serbia to get your special effects done. Remember Building Block Two of my Three Building Blocks (New-Media Technology—Equipment)?

Technology has evolved so much that the projects that used to take teams of talented craftspeople and CGI artists can now be done by a kid on his laptop in his basement. And finding technicians and artists who can do the job you need is easier than ever. You can look for them by screening film-festival winners or by checking out the AFI Student Academy Awards (or any student academy awards) and taking a look at their effects work. Use Box Office Mojo and IMDbPro and its advanced search to find the most recent low-budget science fiction movies. (IMDbPro, an extensive online media database, is the bible of the film, television, and video game industry, with more than one hundred million inquiries per month and climbing.)

Or take the case of Gareth Edwards. He started directing the low-budget, sci-fi, special-effects film *Monsters* with a crew of seven and a budget of $15,000. He completed the film for under $500,000, and although the film was not a critical success, it got the attention of Warner Brothers, and he was then hired by them to shoot their high-budgeted, high-profile *Godzilla* remake.

And getting a special-effects person to work with you may not be as difficult as you think. Sure the search to find the right person is time consuming, but as you can see and will see from the experiences in my career, this type of diligent work pays off. And once you find this person willing to work with you and the ground rules are set—i.e., that it is a labor of love and something to help both your careers—then the rest (price, schedule, etc.) often falls into place quicker than imaginable. It's not hard to negotiate when you have no real money. Either they are interested, or they're not. The only real things you have to negotiate with on a short are credits and accommodating the special-effects person's schedule. But make sure these understandings are written down, preferably with the assistance of an attorney, so that there will be no misunderstandings during the process. Speaking of lawyers and writing things down . . .

The Option to Option

You can also consider optioning material. Optioning material essentially means that if you find something to develop that you have not created or do not own, then you have to get the legal rights to develop that material. You do not actually acquire the material itself outright, but rather you acquire the right (almost all of the time, the *exclusive* right) to acquire the rights to the material at some time in the future. A call to a lawyer would be helpful here.

At certain points in the book I will suggest that you consult with a lawyer. Alarm bells may ring in your head: *But aren't lawyers expensive?* It ain't necessarily so. Here are some suggestions on finding affordable, and at times cost-free, legal advice:

- Volunteer Lawyers for the Arts is a nationwide service that provides free legal advice if you meet their requirements. And if you do not meet their requirements, they can recommend relatively inexpensive legal counsel.
- Independent Film Project is another organization that often can steer you to cost-effective legal counsel.
- American Bar Association referral services exist in many cities and states, and for a reasonable fee.
- The New York City Bar Association charges thirty-five dollars for the first half-hour consultation, and then you can negotiate with them for any additional fees. Often these attorneys, who have been prescreened by the bar, are young and starting out, and can offer very competitive rates.
- Law schools often have legal clinics that specialize in entertainment law, and would be open to help-

ing out young filmmakers. And even if the law
schools near you may not have an entertainment-
law clinic, chances are good that they would have
an intellectual-property professor who may be able
to lead you to some very smart, inexpensive attorneys. You can also approach a nearby law school's
career-placement office and ask them if they can
recommend any starting-out entertainment attorneys in your area.

- Craigslist is another possibility. For twenty-
five dollars you can advertise for an inexpensive
attorney. You'd be surprised how effective this
strategy can be if done properly.

The thing to realize is that many attorneys want to get into
the entertainment field, and if you present yourself as someone
with a promising future, their responses often will surprise
you. In addition, at this stage of your filmmaking career you do
not need much legal support. They can draft initial contracts
for you, and you can use those contracts, varying and revising
them, as needed, in the future by briefly consulting your attorney on their language.

The Case Study in Development That Jump-Started My Career: The Harder You Work, the Luckier You Get

Early in my career, before I had ever produced a
film, I was doing collection calls for a dentist in Jamaica,
Queens. A secretary of one of my office neighbors heard
I had a PhD in mass-media communication. Somehow
that made him think I must be a producer. He had a

friend with an idea for a film. She (Jen Toth) was a reporter for the Washington Post, *and had written a book called* The Mole People: Life in the Tunnels Beneath New York City *about "mole people"—the destitute, downtrodden class of society in New York who actually live underground in the subway system. She thought it would make a great film. I told her I had never produced before, but I could give it my best try. She agreed, and I optioned it for no money. Not really knowing what a producer does, I talked to someone else who rented space on my floor, who I knew was a producer, and asked him to partner with me, which he agreed to do.*

Making a choice to find a producing partner is a difficult one. Often you would like to go it alone. I mean, I found the story; why should I share it with someone fifty-fifty? What do they bring to the relationship? However, I also knew that I admired this producer very much, and he had many contacts in the industry, contacts that I did not have. Based upon the prominence of the book and its unique subject matter, I probably could have set up meetings with the appropriate distributors and end users, but I decided to take the quicker route, giving up 50 percent in return for saving time and learning from a producer whom I really respected.

My partner got us a meeting at HBO through someone he knew. HBO loved the idea and optioned the book from me. I had gone from nothing to producing a movie with HBO simply because my office neighbor's secretary really didn't know what I did for a living.

So I was now a producer, but I had no idea what to do next. My partner told me we needed to find a writer. So I called Miramax. Cold. I gave them my pitch and told them I was looking for someone to write the script.

I told them about the book's success, how HBO thought it was going to be an amazing project, and how great the upside could be for anyone attached. They listened for a few seconds, and then hung up.

So I called Screen Gems. They listened for a few minutes (which was an improvement!), and then they hung up. I called New Line Cinema. And they ignored me. The first time. And then I called a second time and finally found someone who listened. The second New Line executive knew the perfect writer. (Later I would find out that this "perfect person" just happened to be her fiancé.) I read a sample script that he just wrote, really liked his writing style, met with him, and he was the one whom I decided to submit to HBO as the script-writer for our Mole People movie.

There was wind at my back now. I'd attached a New Line Cinema–recommended writer to my HBO project and was now going to turn around and take his writing-sample script to HBO and talk them into using him for our movie. My mojo was rising.

But HBO didn't quite feel the same way about my writer's sample script. They hated it. Really hated it. They hated it so much it made them question their commitment to the original project I brought to them. They now felt my taste was so awful that they actually fired me from the film; that is, HBO decided to no longer work on my project. The HBO executive went as far as telling me, you're a nice, smart guy, but you really have no taste, are not cut out for this business, and should think of another career path.

It was a good lesson and a spectacularly bad mojo miscalculation.

But despite what HBO said, I still liked the writer's original sample script. And a few weeks after being fired, Marlen Hecht (my wife and fellow producer), the writer, his fiancée, and I had dinner. And Marlen, who knew how much I liked and saw potential in the script and agreed with me as such, suggested that we put together the money and make a low-budget independent film. (The writer also had some National Endowment for the Arts grant money for a short film, which we used, and then later paid back to them.)

This was a valuable lesson about trusting my initial instincts about material, because that writer's sample script was Spanking the Monkey, *and the writer was David O. Russell. And had I accepted HBO telling me no, I never would have made the films I've made.*

Now Put Your Idea on Paper: The First Steps Towards Turning Your Idea into an Actual Screenplay

Following the tenets in this chapter, you should now have a list of ideas you are interested in making into a screenplay—and ultimately into a film. Whatever ideas and thoughts you jot down can start out as purely factual, but you eventually must extrapolate from there. And make something attention grabbing, or just plain crazy: if it is a story about three friends growing up in your neighborhood, make one an alien, or the smartest person in the world, or planning a way to off the bully who has been harassing one of them. True life, as interesting as it may sound to you, is often not great fodder for narrative-fiction filmmaking. It could be a starting point, but just that, a *starting* point.

Now show your list of movie ideas to people you know and trust. Pitch a few of your most trusted and respected friends your strongest idea. I know "pitch" sounds like a horrible "industry" word, but there is a method to this madness. If you cannot enthusiastically summarize your idea in just a few paragraphs, chances are you will have real trouble getting it made. Don't get the opinion of just one or two people; pitch to as many trustworthy people as you can. You don't even have to tell them it's a movie you want to write. Just tell them you heard about an upcoming film and give them a quick elevator pitch.

You will start to see a consensus develop—some aspects of your concept will be well received, and others won't. From here you elaborate on what works, expand the good stuff, and—if you start to see a trend—eliminate the concepts that aren't getting a strong response. This is how you develop material—revising it, shaping it, sending it in new directions, but always making it stronger. When the process is over, you will feel much more confident about your screenplay, and your movie will be better (and more successful) for it.

Which segues nicely back to my opening anecdote: meeting Harvey Weinstein at the Miramax offices as I was about to pitch him my film ...

> *I'm walking down the hall to Harvey's office, thinking about the larger-than-life figure that he's become—the way his taste, passion, and aesthetic are absolutely unparalleled. The real secret to his success is his sense of the market and internal gauge of what will sell and what won't. His respect for that aspect of the business was so essential, so primary, that even if he loved your script he'd pass if he didn't see the market for it. Every time.*
>
> *So I made my pitch. I walked into the room, and the first thing I did was to give Harvey Weinstein the finger.*

I launched right into how we could market my movie by describing the poster: a beautiful woman, alone in the middle of a two-lane desert highway, looking directly at the camera and extending her ring finger as a kind of stylized "F.U." The movie was a comedy that dealt with themes of womanhood and expectations of female behavior. The image of a woman pseudo-flipping off the world with her ring finger perfectly captured the essence of the film. It also tapped into a way to market and position the movie—as something irreverent, challenging, sexy, in your face. There hadn't really been a poster like it before. Harvey loved it.

The research we had done in advance let me go into Harvey's office with a marketing concept, a script, and even a poster idea. I walked out of his office with a deal. And a commitment to make the movie Committed *that was worth several million dollars. And guess what poster we used when we marketed the film.* Committed? . . . Yes!

The key lesson here is not that I made a deal; it's how I went about making it. I didn't walk in there with material I knew would knock his socks off and simply try to sell a movie. That's awfully tough sledding. Decision makers like Harvey are hard-wired to say no. It's the safest play for them, since most movies with no attachments are risky propositions. And under normal circumstances, perhaps Harvey would have passed on a film like mine. But I sold a package—a plan, a way to show him why people would see the movie, which in turn helped him see how the movie could be marketed. So he couldn't say no—at least not as easily.

A Few Final Thoughts

No stage of the filmmaking process is easy. You can't coast. Ever. And the development process is no exception.

As for inspiration, ultimately it will come. Hey, I mean, you've already bought this book; that's the first step in showing how committed you are to making a career in the film and television industry. I'm more interested in how that inspiration helps you make the right choices.

And if you can't write it, you can find it. The stories are out there, everywhere around us—in short-story anthologies, YouTube videos, or in some edgy downtown black-box theater.

After you're finished with this book, you'll be looking at a blank page.

But don't worry: If you pay attention to the lessons here, you will face very few blank pages in your life in the film and television industry.

THE SCRIPT

Ladies and Gentlemen . . . Start Your Engines!

Several years ago, I received a call from my dear friend and producer extraordinaire Klaus Volkenborn. He told me he had some funding available from ZDF, a huge, German government–supported television station. I thought this was great, and that maybe we could partner and produce something together. That's what Klaus had in mind too, but he didn't want me solely as a producer. He was calling to see if I'd like to write and direct a low-budget film. Within the next six months.

At this stage of my career, I'd already produced some successful films and was very confident with my skills in that department. But directing? Pretty much the only people I'd ever given direction to were my kids, and even they weren't the easiest to work with (you try waking up two boys at 6:30 a.m. to get them to school on the other side of town). In my heart of hearts I was still a comparative literature/religious studies major who never met a camera he wasn't afraid of.

But who wouldn't be intrigued by the idea of directing their first film? I had actually been playing around with a script idea for quite a few years, so this was the perfect opportunity to check my insecurities at the door and go full throttle ahead.

But where to begin? I had never actually written a script before, much less directed a film. I had no formal training in screenwriting. Sure, by that time I had read and contributed to other people's successful scripts, but this meant starting from scratch because this screenplay wasn't going to write itself. I had to do it.

How was I going to get this all done within the required time frame?

It was a trial by fire. And here's what I learned.

This is not a chapter about how to write the great American screenplay. The media-book landscape is littered with those books. And there is no magic bullet, no secret on how to write a successful script. If that were the case, then there wouldn't be so many books telling you how to write that great script; we'd all just be writing great scripts. So what follows in this chapter is not how to write a great script, but rather how to optimize the chances of getting yourself the strongest script that you can before you start shooting your movie. The good news is that even if you are not comfortable writing your own script at present, as I discussed in chapter 2, you can always option material and work with collaborators on your project. So what follows is just one path, a path based upon what I did to get my script ready for my directorial debut.

The three most important things to focus on when you're just starting the process of developing a film are the script, the script, and the script. And whether you write it or have someone else write it, or if you are a director, actor, writer, or producer, you still must follow the same principles.

You have followed the steps in chapter 2 on developing an idea, so you now have your idea or ideas for your film. But there are other questions you have to ask yourself in the script-making process:

Do I make a short, or a feature film? Once you've solidified your concept, you have to decide whether you want to create a short or feature-length film. Your developed concept often can work as either. As a matter of fact, I have seen many short films later made into full-length feature films. So answering this question has everything to do with where you are on the continuum of your professional growth: If you have done many shorts, you may feel you are ready for a feature—then I would probably advise you to go for it. But, in general, if you are starting out, I recommend a short for a couple of key reasons:

- **Creativity:** Don't be fooled. It is very hard to write and make a great short. As the French mathematician/philosopher Blaise Pascal said, "If I had more time, I would have written you a shorter letter." Think about it—you've got to produce something that is structurally sound, touching, poignant, funny—and all in a tiny narrative window. So the process of working on a short becomes extremely rewarding and self-instructive. Shorts are excellent creative laboratories, and because they can be cheaper to make you are freer to experiment with new ideas without the high stakes associated with missteps and mistakes. Knock yourself out here.

- **Cost** (Building Block Two: New-Media Technology—Equipment): Although shorts can at times cost more than low-budget, full-length feature films, shorts done smartly can be relatively inexpensive to create, so climbing your "learning curve" by making shorts can become very cost-effective. It's a matter of arithmetic—you can make many, many shorts for the price to make one feature film, and each one gives you an opportunity to get seen and to make a creative statement. Everything being equal, the more times up at bat, the greater your chances of success.

But most people go about making shorts the wrong way. That's a competitive advantage for you, because after you finish this book and learn the proper way to make a short film, you will stand out in the marketplace. Where most people fall down in their process has everything to do with the state of our media consumption. We're in the midst of a digital-entertainment revolution. Content is everywhere now, streaming whenever you want it. And because there's so much competition for eyeballs, there's an incentive to create content in quick, bite-sized chunks—material that's easy to watch and easy to digest. (Ever check out 5SecondFilms.com? Or become a Vine.com seven-second filmmaker?) As a result, our attention span grows shorter, so the shorts that filmmakers are making tend to fall into fast, punchy bits like a *Saturday Night Live* skit. They're like a good joke: great for telling at parties, but *not* for learning how to entertain, to tell a story, and to become a filmmaker.

Are craft, luck, and experience enough? Yes. The writer Malcolm Gladwell popularized the theory that you need ten thousand hours of doing something until you become a master at it. While I'm not sure I agree that the number is quite so high, I know from personal experience that he is onto something here. Repetition breeds competence. Doing many shorts and learning from your mistakes on them really does make you a better filmmaker. For example, filmmaker Rian Johnson (*Looper, Brick*) always said that he's made many, many short films before he started making feature films. There's no magic number, no amount of shorts that will get you over a certain artistic threshold as a filmmaker. You're not guaranteed to get exposure and film and television opportunities, but you are absolutely finding your voice and bending the curve in your favor by making as many shorts as you can.

Or look at Lena Dunham, creator of the HBO series *Girls*. Did you know that her first short film starred her little sister as an art dealer, then two web series followed, then a very low-budget film entitled *Creative Nonfiction*, and then another very low-budget feature, *Tiny Furniture*, before getting *Girls* made and breaking into television?

Should I collaborate, write the screenplay by myself, or have someone write it for me? There is no right answer here. Not everyone wants to (or can) write their own screenplay. If you don't want to write, that's okay, just bring someone in to write for you, following the guidelines I suggest for hiring in chapter 6. Furthermore, be aware that if you do want to write or cowrite, and if you are also directing, producing, or acting in your film, the creative burden may be too great, particularly if it's your first time out. I say this from a practical as well as creative point of view. And obviously if you are also making a full-length feature as opposed to a short film, the level of difficulty of doing more things at the same time raises the bar even higher.

Pauline Kael, the longtime film critic for *The New Yorker*, once wrote that a major reason films aren't as good as they used to be is that years ago producers had more clout. Back then producers weren't just money raisers; they were an integral part of the creative process. Producers used to be a creative force shaping the artistic contours of their projects, and had a much stronger collaborative relationship with their film directors. She argues that this kind of creative relationship made the ultimate product better. And perhaps she's right—that producer-director give-and-take has diminished even further over the years. So as you start out in your career, don't always think that you have to do it all; a strong producer can be an invaluable addition to your team.

To begin with, make sure that when you come up with your original idea, you immediately copyright it with the United States Copyright office (www.copyright.gov). You can copyright it online, and it is a relatively inexpensive and easy procedure. Working specifically with writing collaborators can be a dicey proposition. Jealousies can arise. In my years of working as a lawyer in the industry, the most common source of friction between collaborators stems from arguments over whose contribution was more vital to the success of the creative endeavor. Because everyone thinks it was theirs. That's why it's *absolutely vital* that before you begin collaborating with anyone, you have some kind of legal agreement in place—even a simple one that lays out expectations and understandings for the project. I'd say that about 65 to 75 percent of the problems I have encountered as an entertainment attorney for my clients have been about issues of who did what, and who owns the copyright to the end product.

So please, get your collaboration understanding in writing. And make sure that your collaboration agreement gives you sole right to your idea, and that your collaborator is working for you, so if the collaboration does not work out, you still own the idea and concept, and can go forward without any major future obstacles.

Five, Four, Three, Two, One, GO!

You now know if you are shooting a short or feature film, you know your genre, and you are ready to either collaborate or option and have someone else write for you, or write yourself.

As mentioned, there are a zillion books on screenwriting: how to do it, when to do it, how to get beyond writer's block, etc. One thing I've learned is that there are as many successful approaches to screenwriting as there are successful screen-writers.

Your first rule of screenwriting is that you don't talk about the rules of screenwriting (okay, okay, all you *Fight Club* fans got that reference, I know, too easy). But in reality, as Robert McKee writes in *Story*, there are no hard-and-fast rules in screenwriting, just principles to follow.

So here are six principles that are essential.

The First Principle: A Screenplay Is a Unique Format

Unlike a novel or short story, where the rules of structure and rhythm are open-ended, a movie can't be much less than eighty-five minutes, and (in today's market) is rarely longer than two hours. Short films can range from five minutes to approximately forty-five minutes. Most screenplays simply cannot be successful if they don't have the classic three-act structure, sticking pretty closely to necessary rhythms of rising action and building drama. Even most shorts need to follow this basic paradigm if they're going to tell a story.

You can find the parameters of the three-act structure online and in the many books on screenwriting. There are numerous variations on this theme for television and film, but essentially it says that a film's story is comprised of three acts, usually playing out over a two-hour time period. Please remember that these structures are flexible; it is easy to fall into following these principles *too* precisely. Do *not* do this. Just start writing, take stock of what you have, and only then look to how it might fit into this general outline:

1. Act 1 (thirty minutes) includes an inciting incident in the first few minutes, culminating in a major plot movement at the end of the first act, where the protagonist takes on the problem created by the inciting incident.

2. Act 2 (sixty minutes), in which the protagonist attacks the problem, and changes his or her character (the "character arc") to attempt to overcome the obstacles, as all characters become more clearly defined and developed.

3. Act 3 (thirty minutes), where the protagonist's conflict reaches its climax, and then is resolved with all the major characters reaching a new understanding of who they are.

When I started writing my screenplay for *The Atlantis Conspiracy*, the first thing I did was read a few books on the three-act structure until I felt I had a comfortable understanding of it. I then went about crafting my story in this form—creating a protagonist, an inciting incident in act 1, the character development in act 2, and the resolution in act 3.

Of course, a complete understanding of the rules will help you learn how powerful it can sometimes be to break them. You can't be a slave to structure. You can't get caught up in page counts and act breaks, and rewrite your script because your "inciting incident" happens a few pages from where the latest screenwriting book says it needs to be. In truth there really are no rules, just principles, which is paramount to remember. So sure, listen to the "rules," but also break or bend them when appropriate. Take chances. Play with extreme ideas. And be aware that you're competing in an extraordinarily crowded marketplace.

And again, the Internet is a bounty of information on screenwriting. Start reading screenplays (which can also be found online)—good ones, bad ones. See how they work; match their story rhythms to the theoretical script frameworks you've researched. It's a great way to learn how to develop your script.

In my particular case of starting to write *The Atlantis Conspiracy,* once I understood the three-act structure and filled it in with my specific story, I then sought ways to deviate from this form. For example, I was making a thriller and I decided to create an inciting incident that was not readily recognizable in the opening few minutes of the script. And I hoped to keep the viewer's attention by not revealing the inciting incident in the first few pages, but rather slowly revealing it through the development of the characters and the action of the plot within the first twenty to twenty-five pages of my script.

The Second Principle: It Starts with Story and Characters

Since it all begins with the story and its characters, it becomes self-evident that to start with the best foundation, you have to create the most interesting and memorable scenarios and characters possible. But I am constantly amazed at how often first-time screenplay writers ignore this fundamental principle, how many times I read a sad, dysfunctional, coming-of-age screen-play from these first-time writers.

How did I find my storyline? I started combing newspapers, magazines, etc., looking for interesting scenarios to create for my script. It was more than ten years ago, and what caught my eye were the beginnings of an ecology-based business industry—the corporate "greening" of America. I knew that this would be a very interesting growth industry, so I decided to place my story in this arena.

I then set about creating my protagonist against the back-drop of an activist ecological construction company. And who better to lead this company than a strong, ideologically commit-ted woman? Add to this mix her husband and their best friend, and you have the beginnings of a provocative and unusual story.

Once you set up your interesting characters and environ-ment, you can then go about finding your theme. In this case it was the disillusionment of an idealist, and how you can try to rediscover your idealism in the real world.

And once you find your theme, your plot should follow suit: I devised a plot to my theme and environment that involves a husband who commits suicide, a questionable best friend, an eccentric sidekick, and the FBI investigating your idealistic company. I was now ready to write my screenplay.

Jim Mangold, a wonderful director and writer (*The Wolverine* and *Walk the Line*) whom I worked with, used to talk about his theory of "triangulation," which means that an ideal scene should combine and advance three things in it: the char-acter, the theme, and the plot. It's something that has always remained with me, which has proven to be a formidable goal in each scene I write.

I did not write the next *Godfather*, and there are many screenplays I would have written differently now, but through thoughtful research I was able to optimize the possibilities of success on a screenplay for my directorial debut by starting out creating interesting characters in an interesting environment with a plot that tied in with my theme—a script that I was eager to shoot.

Another example of the importance of having interesting characters and a theme "finding" their plot is the film *Frozen River.* Courtney Hunt, the writer/director of that film, originally approached me with a script titled *Mohawk Bingo,* about a single mother of two boys who resorted to smuggling cigarettes across the Canadian border to the United States in order to make ends meet.

While I was working with her on her script, I had happened to read an article about the smuggling of illegal immigrants into the United States, and I then suggested to her to change her plot from smuggling in cigarettes to smuggling in illegal immigrants. This change would make the struggle more powerful and more connected to the personal travails and themes of the protagonist and her cohorts. She listened, she changed the story from smuggling cigarettes to illegal immigrants, and the film went on to gain major success, including being nominated for two Oscars (including Best Original Screenplay).

I am not saying that my idea made the film into a hit, but it did help enhance and strengthen the ties between the characters, the theme, and the plot, and helped optimize the film's chances for success.

The Third Principle: We All Begin at the Same Starting Line

Don't be afraid. Don't think you can't do it, or even can't oversee the process. There's a good chance that most of your initial work will be bad. It happens with almost all first timers. Don't let it discourage you, because you're going to learn how to make it better. Filmmaker David Lynch, a major proponent of experimental filmmaking and distribution, said in the documentary *Side by Side* that amidst all this new and overwhelming technology, remember this: It's still an even playing field. "We all start out," he said, "with the same blank piece of paper and pen in front of us."

The Fourth Principle: Change Is Good

My filmmaking partner, Marlen Hecht, often reminds me of an old adage: A single film is made and remade many times—first when you write it, then when you shoot it, and finally when you edit it together. So keep this in mind while writing your screenplay. You can't be too precious and inflexible; it will change innumerable times before it is finally screened.

The Fifth Principle: Every Script Is Different

There is no set way to begin writing your script. I just completed writing a science-fiction road film with comic elements (what a surprise, right?) for a film that I intend to direct in the coming year.

I had a good deal of trouble getting started on writing this script. I tried following the principles I had followed on *The Atlantis Conspiracy,* but it just wasn't working. Then I paused to ask, what had inspired me to write this particular screenplay? It was the unusual characters and the specific storyline twist. So that's what I wrote first—I wrote the scene with the storyline twist, and then a few random scenes that I had envisioned for my characters when I initially came up with the idea. No order, no three-act structure, no triangulation, etc.—just scenes. But it worked.

Once I had written these scenes, everything else then fell into place. Now that I saw my characters in action in prominent scenes, I was able to solidify my theme. Then, with theme in hand and some key scenes written, I slowly created my three-act structure and wrote the screenplay. A very different process than my writing *The Atlantis Conspiracy,* but it was the right one for me at that particular time and place.

The Sixth Principle: A Script Is Not a High School Essay

Most of us have been trained as students to come to school, sit down, and write a creative essay, which we will be graded on. Creative writing doesn't work that way. Don't read these principles and then sit down and try to write your screenplay. It may take you weeks or months, and it will *not* be started and completed in one sitting. Inspiration comes in many different forms, and at many different times, and in many different pieces.

Theories of Creativity

Whether you are writing something original, writing something based upon existing material, or overseeing a hired collaborator, these same principles should apply in each case. But how do you create in a way that's going to ensure you get what you want and need?

Although there's no magic creative pill or mysterious hidden switch to flip, I want to offer up some ideas, gleaned from successful artists, and from extremely helpful habits I have picked up over the years.

Ritual/Habit

I like the famous choreographer Twyla Tharp's notion that creativity is a muscle—and the more you exercise, strengthen, and feed that muscle, the stronger it becomes. That means constant activity, until the act of strengthening that muscle becomes ritual and habit to you. Once something becomes a habit, there is no turning back. It just becomes part of you.

I exercise almost every day. Some days it is very hard to get motivated, but I follow a specific habit every morning, and when I put on my left sneaker first and tie the laces, something almost mechanical kicks in. Without even really thinking about it, I'm on my way and out the door.

A major part of our day is spent doing habit-forming activities. Recent studies have shown that—whether the conscious mind is involved or not—the brain wants to make habits. It likes habits. It takes less energy to act in a way that you have before than it does to invent a new way to go about doing things. You probably brush your teeth the same way every day, shave the same way every day, dry off from the shower following the same pattern every day. Because it's easier.

If the brain is wired that way, why not take advantage of this? A good professional basketball player follows a very specific ritual before he takes a free throw, when he warms up before the game, and when he shoots free throws during the game.

You have to develop those kinds of patterns when you create and write. Set up very specific rituals: Write at the same time, in the same place, always get a cup of coffee in your favorite mug, always have music—or never have music. Whatever you do, be consistent. And then follow that ritual every day while you are writing. Pretty soon it will become your greatest habitual asset. It all becomes automatic.

As with most things in life, with a positive comes a negative. Habit is a wonderful thing, but recent studies have *also* shown that habit tends to stultify creativity. As mentioned, the brain yearns for habit because it is the easy way out. When you form habits, your brain goes on autopilot. It does not grow; it actually loses elasticity, resulting in loss of brainpower.

So what to do?

The answer lies between two extremes. Keep the preliminary rituals of your established habits of creativity and writing, but in other aspects of your life, actually go out of your way to break habits. Shake things up. Improvise. Ad-lib.

I will always keep the ritual of tying my left sneaker first, because that gets me out the door to exercise every day, but I will always mix up the exercises I am doing—change their order, change what I do every day, change where I exercise, etc. You can keep your creative rituals, but mix up the other subtle habits you may not have even realized your brain has created over the years. Brush your teeth with your other hand. Eat an apple in a way you never have before. Wake up and get ready for your day in a completely different order.

When I taught at New York University graduate school, a colleague, the wonderful and internationally renowned professor Neil Postman, once told me the secret to his successful and prolific writing career. He said he would write every morning at a specific time at a diner in his neighborhood (note the habit/ritual!), so he would have no distractions. This forced him to write, and whenever he would find himself stalling, he would change diners ("the mix-up")!

Memory

Your memory is an excellent repository of creativity. There are aspects of the human mind that are intimately connected. It makes perfect sense: the stronger your memory—your store-house of facts, knowledge, and arcana—the more material you have to draw from in your writing.

More specifically, having a strong memory is essential to creating the strongest screenplay. Not only is it helpful to have a good memory for tracking all of the characters, plots, themes, etc., but it's enormously helpful for solving screenplay problems. I can't tell you how many times I've used a funny line that I heard in a fleeting moment from my past because it remained in my head. Or how many times some obscure reference in a book or magazine article helped inspire a plot twist because it stuck in my head. Improving the skill of accessing your store-house of information can be hugely influential in the process of screenwriting.

Maybe you remember something strange a weird kid said to you in your third-grade class that would be an amazing line for a character, or a plot twist in one of *The Canterbury Tales* that you can translate to your story, or something to help a protagonist out of a hopeless situation—like how an internal combustion engine works. The stronger your memory, the easier it becomes to tap into your creativity. So an important creative goal is to keep on strengthening your memory and to create memory habits as well. I have seen prominent writer clients of mine do many things in this realm. Here are ways to improve your memory:

1. If you have an iPod, try to memorize the order of the songs you have heard when walking or exercising.

2. Go see a movie and enter at the halfway mark, watch it to the end, and then immediately watch the beginning of the next showing of that film. You'll find that your brain now approaches film in a fascinating and counterintuitive manner.

3. Balance is a major factor in enhancing memory power. Practice balancing on one foot, and then on the other. This might sound crazy, but studies are pretty emphatic on this point.

4. Play trivia games online (particularly about things you do not know).

5. There are many excellent books available about strengthening your memory; research them, read them, and practice their exercises.

E. B. White once said, "Habitually creative people are prepared to be lucky." It's all about continuous creative exercise and memory-muscle building. That's the gate opener. Then the rest is up to you.

Practical Creativity: Writing and Overseeing Writing

Fail as often as you can. I cannot overemphasize the importance of failure as a pathway to success. You see and hear this everywhere: You cannot possibly succeed without failing first and learning from your failures along the way. That thought should be self-evident, but as we exist in such a success-driven society, it can be hard to remember that failure is a key component of the creative process.

The first draft of your screenplay won't always be great. That's a failure. The first rough cut of your movie will be too long and uninteresting. Failure again. And your first completed short will also have flaws and failures. You can see the pattern. But those failures are necessary because they put you in position to rewrite, recut, and rethink how and why you failed. It also allows you to improve your skills and create something superior the next time around.

The story in *The King's Speech* is ideally emblematic of this "failure" truth. King George VI learned that unless he put himself out there, kept trying and faltering and then picking himself up and starting again, he would have nowhere to go. Failure is the cornerstone to success. More on this later.

Write with actors in mind. I am not saying that you have to have that actor when you shoot your film, but many of the writers I have worked with tell me that if they visualize a particular actor or actors for particular roles, that helps enormously in their writing. When I was writing *The Atlantis Conspiracy*, I had a specific actress in mind for the lead. Although I did not end up using that actress, the visualization of her during my screenwriting process proved to be enormously helpful.

Rewrites: Get that muscle going. Everyone says that "writing is rewriting" because it's absolutely true. Most people's first drafts are seriously flawed—even those of big Hollywood screenwriters. So how do you make them better? Rewriting. And rewriting. And rewriting. I lost count of how many rewrites were conducted by filmmakers I've worked with so far.

Table reads, table reads, table reads. Doing a "table read," where people come together to read and constructively criticize your work as a group, is one of the most important, economical, and overlooked things you can do in maximizing the creative potential of your product. At first blush you may think we are getting way ahead of ourselves in doing table reads when you are in the beginnings of writing your script. But this is *exactly* when you should be doing table reads—when you are in the process of writing your screenplay.

Writing a screenplay is an ongoing, "non-precious" process, and a table read can and should be done early on, to make sure you are on the right track. This is your first step to introduce your work to the public at large. Then go from there. Many times in my career, when I felt lost while working on a screenplay, I had numerous table reads throughout the rewriting process (most without trained actors), which turned out to be one of the most valuable exercises I did.

So accept it, be terrified of it, and then rejoice in it, because:

1. It's effective: When you get your friends together to have them read your work out loud, you will be shocked by how many interesting things come from yourself and your participants. Hearing performers interpret your lines with emphasis and intention that is perhaps different from how you saw the film is one of the most revealing exercises you can put your script through. And the readers don't have to be brilliant—even if your friends are not the best actors, just the process of you hearing the words spoken aloud outweighs any deficiencies in the performances. And it's great practice for the real deal—the more you become familiar with your work, the greater command you'll have over it, and the more you'll be ready when it comes time to start preproduction. Giving feedback to and getting

feedback from actors is no different than any other skill—the more practice you have, the better and more comfortable you'll be at it.

2. You simultaneously start building your team. By working with other people on your script, you start to figure out who is helpful to your vision and who is not. These are the first steps in finding your collaborators as you build your vision and career. I know that I found many future collaborators in doing my table reads.

3. It's inexpensive: You can do it over and over again, with minimal cost, and maximum potential for learning new things about your work. And the beauty of a table read is that it remains as effective a tool at *every* stage in the process of developing your script, whether you're finessing it through the writing phase, or even when you've already begun preproduction. On a few occasions in my career, when a shoot was not going well, I actually called a table read *during* production to figure out what wasn't working—a little like an on-the-fly theatrical workshop. While I don't recommend doing this for the fainthearted, it has proven an effective tactic nonetheless.

A caveat: something to be very aware of. Sometimes people feel that they have to be critical because they were brought in to find things wrong with your script. So they search for flaws to validate your trust in their opinion and justify their value to the process.

And at the same time, some people are so excited to be part of the process, and want you to be happy, that they say only positive things—which really isn't that helpful either. I remember a prominent studio executive once telling me that you can really "die of encouragement" in this industry. No one wants to say anything negative because they don't want to hurt your feelings, and if their ideas turn out to be "wrong," they will be embarrassed they didn't see the value of your work. So why take a chance and say anything negative? I have been to many, many table reads, and I have never heard a negative consensus. Sure there were pockets of criticism, but the consensus has always been positive, which is not a great thing—it doesn't give your script what it needs.

This aspect of the process can be very onerous for me. I am always open to listening to others, so at times it becomes difficult for me to separate the "wheat from the chaff."

The answer? Always look for consensuses. Sure it's nice to hear good things, but you have to have confidence in your work. If one character or sequence or plot device keeps getting flagged by readers over and over again, chances are you need to address it. And if certain people are always part of that consensus—they seem to be true barometers of where your script is at—I would look towards them as key members of the team you want to build as you move towards production.

At the end of the day, always remember, this is your film. Somali musician K'naan relates an old fable about a fox: This fox had a remarkably beautiful walk, for which every animal in town adored him. One day the fox saw a prophet stride gloriously into town. The fox decided to improve on his own beautiful way of walking by copying the way the prophet walked. He started to imitate the prophet, but ultimately could not match his walk exactly. Worse still, he suddenly forgot his own unique way of walking, and the fox was left with nothing, and that's why foxes walk in the unremarkable way that they walk nowadays.

Consensus or not, you must know yourself instinctually. Know what works for you. Of course you will make mistakes following your instinct, but the more you use it in conjunction with everything else in this chapter, the more effective it becomes for you, and you become your most trusted ally in the creative process.

> *And what happened to my script and film for ZDF and Klaus Volkenborn?*
>
> *I used all the lessons in this chapter: I did my research, I created what I hoped were interesting characters and environments that tied in well with my theme and plot. I did many table reads and many rewrites after those table reads and after constructive criticism from my colleagues. And then I had my script completed and ready for production.*
>
> *I wrote and directed* The Atlantis Conspiracy, *which I sold to HBO. It won some awards, and it still gets many views on Netflix and other streaming sites. It is still playing in Germany and other countries, many years after its original release.*

As you are beginning to see, there is a counterintuitive world out there that exists for you to find. Be different, take advantage of that difference, and succeed with it.

Now onward to actually making your movie.

DEVELOPMENT AND ACTORS

This Is Your Role Too!

I had worked as an attorney with a prominent actor who was getting older, and was no longer getting the roles she had traditionally gotten. She had starred in a very popular television series, and in many movies as well. It was now a very frustrating time for her. She could do amazing accents, play different ethnicities, and created inventive, quirky characters, but no one knew that wonderful side of her talent. I urged her to make a short film that showed her playing an amazing hodgepodge of unconventional characters, each one with a different, flawlessly performed accent. She resisted. She still wasn't getting work.

I then decided to really push it, to tell her that I may resign as her attorney unless she made this short. That fateful day soon came. Did she make the short? If she did, was it successful?

We'll get back to that a little later.

This is for you actors, so please pay attention (yes, someone is finally paying attention to the struggling actor). Obviously you are one of the most important pieces to any production and yet all too often you are overlooked in the process of making films. And because more often than not you are an after-thought, the actions you have been told to take to "make it" in the industry make absolutely no sense whatsoever, more so now than ever in today's new digital-media environment. But if there's no one on the screen, then you don't have a movie, you have a screensaver.

It's difficult for anyone trying to make it in the film and television business, but actors in particular may have it the toughest—you have been given exactly the same "inside the box" advice for more than fifty years: Take acting courses, get a headshot, and then try to audition for as many roles as possible, and hope to be discovered. It's pretty much what every strug-gling actor everywhere has been told to do. Whereas the rest of the entertainment industry is starting to pay some attention to our new-media environment, the acting industry seems to be stuck in a time warp.

It gets worse for you—even the Screen Actors Guild-American Federation of Television and Radio Artists (SAG-AFTRA) can be a barrier; you will not even be able to audition for any of the good films out there if you are not a member of SAG-AFTRA. And it is very difficult to become a member to begin with, so you end up being caught within a loop of frustration.

I say all of this sitting on the other side of the casting-call fence. As a producer, writer, and director who has led thou-sands of auditions, here's a fact that some of you may know, and some of you may not know, and some of you may wish to ignore: By the time you are the nineteenth or twentieth audi-tion of the day, it all starts to become a blur to the people who are auditioning you. The procession of faces, headshots, and performances—no matter how earnest—all start to bleed together. For starters, headshots I get at an audition or in the mail don't have much meaning or assist in helping me create an impression of you, nor are they a good means of getting my attention. It's more like that old Mitch Hedberg joke about the person handing out leaflets on the street corner: "Whenever I walk, people try to hand me flyers. And when someone tries to hand me a flyer, it's kinda like they're saying, 'Here, you throw this away.'"

And the emotional toll of countless rejections obviously makes the life of an actor that much harder. There is nothing more emotionally debilitating than sitting around hearing actors tell you how difficult it is to break into this industry. And to add to this adverse state of being in the acting industry, acting schools are not yet 100 percent prepared for this new Three Building Blocks universe.

What's the alternative?

By now you realize that the Three Building Blocks have changed everything. As a matter of fact, classic "career development" is clearly dead in this new universe.

So, actors, a new door has been opened for you that you are not normally aware of. Actors are used to being "tread upon," but I'm saying something very radically different right now: It should and can be just the opposite.

You have the skills to empower yourself and move your career forward. I am not going to give you tips on how to become a better actor; that is not what this book is about. But I am going to give you tips on how to use your acting talent in our new-media environment as a means of propelling your career.

This chapter will be the most important chapter you as an actor will ever read in helping determine your career success.

Here's how you do it:

Either direct, write, and/or produce a film or short film starring yourself.

Or if you have an idea for a film or short film, find someone to write and/or direct it, with you playing the lead role.

Yes, make a film starring yourself.

When I look at aspiring new filmmakers, I look for their ability to understand character, story, pacing, timing, and mood. And who knows that better than a strong actor? It is not just coincidence that some of our best directors started out as actors.

I produced a film, *The Last Good Time*. It was directed by Bob Balaban, a prominent, Oscar-nominated, experienced, smart, and wonderful actor. And I was amazed at how well he knew which actors to cast, and then how to direct them. He could speak the language, and was truly keyed into how to help get the cast to the places and performances they needed to go to, which was clearly paramount in helping him create a strong, compelling story in his film.

Same thing with Matt Greenberg, a wonderfully talented writer (*1408, Beowulf*) I worked with: He began as an actor in England, and then changed course and decided to become a writer. And it quickly became very clear that his background as an actor was invaluable to his craft and present-day success as a well-known screenwriter.

I also have had the occasion a few times in my career to ask directors to take a basic acting class before they start shooting their first films. And every time they took this class they came back much stronger directors. If a director learns more about directing from actors, then the move from acting to directing shouldn't be as difficult for you as you may think.

So actors, all the advice I give filmmakers in making their first film is directly aimed at you as well. There is nothing to stop you from following my advice and making your first film. You have all the requisite tools; do not be afraid to expand your horizons. And by making your first film you are showcasing your talent both as an actor and a filmmaker, so I have increased your career options by 100 percent. Once you do this, you will join a long list of actors, including Matt Damon, Penny Marshall, Ben Affleck, Zach Braff, Ben Stiller, Will Ferrell, Owen Wilson, Clint Eastwood, Sacha Baron Cohen, and Jason Segal.

You may have heard this advice, but have trepidations about how to proceed, and most important, how to do it well. After reading this book, you won't have this problem.

What's the first step on this path to making your own film?

Know Thyself as an Actor (for the Time Being)

Look at yourself, and decide what type of actor you are. Are you a comedian? Are you "the bad guy" type? The "wacky neighbor" type? This involves some real introspection on your part, and advice from friends and peers who know you and your work.

I am not saying that you will always have to play in only a narrow band of roles, but when starting out, like it or not, you will be "typed." So rather than get angry about this, play to your strengths, use them to your benefit, knowing that when you succeed, you will gain the freedom to change those perceptions.

Once you've identified the kinds of roles that suit you— your "persona"—you can follow the plan and career road map I've laid out in this book and produce a film starring yourself in this specific persona. Do you want to write and/or direct it as well? Fine. And make as many films as you can; then you can add them to your actor's reel, or you can keep your films separate from your actor's reel—the choice is yours.

Vin Diesel knew that his strengths were his mixed nationality and muscular physique, so in 1995 he wrote, directed, produced, and starred in a short, *Multi-Facial,* which Steven Spielberg saw and which led him to cast Vin in *Saving Private Ryan* . . . and the rest is history.

The end result is that once again, as opposed to waiting around for someone to give you validation, you are seizing control and doing it yourself.

Recently, a woman approached me after one of my seminars. She was full of enthusiasm, ready to conquer the world, having just moved to New York from the Midwest to begin her career as an actress. She was very excited, telling me that she had already taken my advice before even hearing me speak, and was starring in a horror movie that she was producing. She had spent a good deal of time putting together her group of trusted collaborators and found an experienced director—someone who had already made seven low-budget horror movies. She was eager to begin. So she was already moving in the right direction; she knew she had to make her own movie starring herself.

But it is more than just taking that first step—it has to be taking the *right* first step. And that's when I gently read her the riot act: Horror movies are virtually useless for creating an acting career. Can you name any actor who broke into the industry in recent years making a low-budget horror movie? Granted the films on occasion do well, but the actors in them don't. In addition, I wasn't impressed that this director had made seven low-budget horror movies. The market is glutted with cheap horror movies, so it takes something extraordinary to break out. This director's track record (seven "nonbreakouts" in a row) didn't sound like he was exactly on the cusp of the next *Paranormal Activity*.

So where could this actor go from here? We reviewed her acting skills and tried to figure out her acting "persona." She was freshly scrubbed from the Midwest, and as she regaled me with wonderful stories of her moving to New York, it became apparent that she should make a comic film about "being a fish out of water" in NYC.

She is now combing the literary universe to find unique stories about a Midwestern "fish out of water," and she will either find one and option and develop it, or write one herself, or collaborate on it with someone else. It was wonderful that she was making her own movie, but her biggest issue in her rush to empower herself was that she did not pause to take the time to "know herself" (for at least the time being).

Your Acting Reel

Another path that should be taken simultaneously with creating your own films is to make the strongest acting reel possible. But be aware: Putting together your acting reel is separate from making your film, and it involves an entirely different set of variables.

When making your own film you control your own destiny, so you self-evaluate and choose the role you think will benefit you most. When making your acting reel, you are creating something for someone else out of a lot of material that you auditioned for and do not control, so obviously you do not have that same amount of autonomy. With your films you are specific and can cast a narrow net, but with your acting reel you have to be general and should cast the widest net possible.

Show your range, but first highlight the type of role you think you're best at. Often people watching your reel don't make it past the first two minutes.

What you need is a good acting reel, one that's polished, professional, and shows range and ability (again, as opposed to the specific acting you do in your own film). Casting directors, producers, and directors are smart and savvy; they want as much information about someone before they cast them.

Do not make your reel open to the public. It makes you look desperate, and you can easily be made fun of. Always use video sites that offer a private option (such as YouTube) or require a password (such as Vimeo).

So when you put together your acting reel, don't be precious about auditioning and only audition for blue-chip productions. Try out for any role you can get in any legitimate film. Shorts, student films, freebies. Particularly if you live in a city that is a media center, there is an entire universe of this kind of work being done all the time. The beauty here is that it doesn't matter if the film or filmmaker isn't great, because, for one of the few times in your life, building your reel is really only about you. As long as you can capture a good performance for you to edit into your acting reel, there is no downside. And although you might get frustrated at the level of competence with some of the directors, the ends do justify the means here. Find the roles. Land the roles. Do professional work. Get the footage. Rinse and repeat.

And if your acting reel is thin, you can add performances from the films you are making to your acting reel, which is a way to try to wrestle back a little more control of your material when it goes out to the marketplace. But know that blending your specific persona from the films you've made with the general roles you've taken in other people's films is a delicate balance; edit your acting reel to be clear about these two distinct paths that you have taken. If balanced well, an actor's reel like this can really get the attention of casting directors, directors, and producers. You'll learn in chapters 8 and 9 how to get those reels to the right people.

Your reel is like a stand-up comedian's act: The goal is to keep adding in new material, change things up, and constantly test things out in order to see what works best.

> *Remember that actor I pushed into making that short film highlighting her ability to do quirky, inventive accents?*
>
> *It worked. She started her short but didn't even have to finish it. People around town heard about it, called her in for "accented" roles, and saw a new side of her, and currently, in addition to the growing film roles she books, she has become one of the major animation/ voice-over stars in Hollywood, starring in movies and television for Disney, Warner Brothers, and Marvel Entertainment.*

You may not be an experienced actor in the entertainment industry, but realize that she got her new career "break" without even completing her short film. By taking control of her career and merely creating a different perception of her skills, she was able to attract attention in an entirely new way, which helped launch her new career in the entertainment industry.

I have seen and heard more and more stories like this starting to happen, particularly in the last few years. However, some actors are producing inexpensive web series with them playing a lead role.

Right general idea, wrong specific execution.

I urge you instead to initially consider directing a short. It is too easy to produce a web series, and very often the quality of these series is compromised and ineffective in your progress. People just rent or buy a cheap digital camera, shoot their friends, edit it together, or keep it as is, and then put it on the web. Because the barrier to entry here is so low, people often don't pay enough attention to making it a great web series; they are just happy to say, "Hey, I have a series on the web I just made." And it shows.

So rather than furthering your career, producing a web series starring you may actually hinder it if it is poorly or thoughtlessly executed. A web series demands a new episode each week. What you're really doing is creating a bunch of badly made television episodes with cliff-hangers that more than likely no one will watch after the first episode because it's too much of a time commitment, and they would rather watch real television. Always choose quality over quantity: You'll be more noticed as an actor in one really good short film than in a series of bad web episodes.

And when you do make your short, don't make it just a group of actors sitting around and acting out monologues. That's the first thing actors may want to do, but the last thing most audiences want to see.

If you are going to work diligently making your own product, you have to strategize how you can maximize this product, even before you've started creating it. Then make it and get it in the hands of the right people. This book will show you step-by-step how to do this.

Many good things will happen when you make your film starring you and when you get your material out into the marketplace.

1. Casting directors and the powers that be will see you in a new light. I can speak from personal experience—when I audition an actor who has directed or written his or her own film, that actor stands out from the

other actors. Even if I have not seen the film, the fact that this person did this is significant on its own and makes me pay more attention.

2. Directing yourself, if done properly, can help you become a better actor. Again, this is not a chapter on how to become a better actor, but it is common sense that the more you direct yourself and the more honest you are about the criticism you get from others and from yourself, the more your acting will improve.

3. Even if you do not have immediate success with your first film, you will have a great time and feel incredibly empowered by making it. It will definitely be worth the experience. And if executed correctly, this will be the first of many films you will create.

4. By continually making your own films, you will become part of a community of like-minded people (e.g., self-motivated directors, writers, and producers), thereby enhancing your positive experience and expanding your connections and horizons in the entertainment industry.

So as you continue to read this book, note that every time you read the advice for filmmakers, I am talking to you, the actor, as well. Actor, filmmaker . . . the words are interchangeable in our new Three Building Blocks universe.

In the "new" Hollywood, for the very first time, actors are in a stronger position than ever before and have more autonomy in pushing their career forward.

That had never been realized, until now.

FUNDRAISING

Show Me the Money!

I had just gotten out of law school and moved back to New York City. I was living in a $186-a-month, fifth-floor studio walk-up in Forest Hills, Queens. I was young and had absolutely no idea what to do with my life. So being the driven person that I was, I got a job making bill-collection phone calls for my law school friend's dentist father in Jamaica, Queens.

One day, after a long shift of working the phones, I decided to unwind in a steam room at my gym before heading back to work later that day. The person next to me struck up a conversation and asked me what I did for a living. I mentioned my background (lawyer and a PhD in mass-media communication), and all of a sudden he jumped up and exclaimed, "Oh, you must be a producer! Just what I was looking for!" He didn't seem to care that I didn't know what a producer was, because he just happened to be looking for one, and oddly enough, I "fit the bill." (I guess it's a universal formula: steam room + media degree = producer.)

*This is one of the things that is so amazing about the entertainment industry. Everyone in it is looking for a producer to help them create their media project, but no one really knows what a producer does. Countless articles have been written on allegedly what a producer does, and countless articles will continue to be written, and with our constantly shifting media environment, a producer's ill-defined role will keeping eluding a definition. When I am asked what a producer does, my answer is this—**a producer protects the vision of the director.** Simple, to the point, and it should be never-changing.*

But to this ill-informed and apparently desperate man, since I was one of the few people in the country who had both a legal degree and a PhD in mass media, I must be a producer. Indeed, a blend of his inexperience and my naïveté.

I should have seen the warning signs.

But I was pretty much done with my steam bath, and as I sat there in the thick, humid air, I realized I could either sit there, continue to prune up, and listen to this guy tell me I was a producer, or head back to my five-flight walk-up, hit the phones, and hassle a few more patients for root-canal payments. He was looking to hire a producer. For money. I decided the patients could wait.

It turned out he was an account executive at an advertising agency, and they had a client who sponsored an annual summer syndicated rock-and-roll concert television series. He told me that the main hosts and producers (all pretty high-profile entertainers) were leaving the series, but the sponsor said they would continue the show, if they could find a new producer and production team.

That's where I came in. Although I told the advertising exec I wouldn't know how to produce myself out of a paper bag, much less a rock-and-roll concert series, he told me not to worry, that I didn't have to actually produce the series; all I had to do was license already produced concert footage that he would then air on television. I was not yet an entertainment lawyer, but I knew I could figure out how to write a license agreement for rock-and-roll footage (although Building Block One [the Internet] didn't exist as it does today; it existed in another format and was called a "library"). So all I had to do was a bit of research, find already existing concert footage to license to air on television, and then execute a few contracts.

And that was my entrée into the entertainment industry.

This producing thing looked like a pretty good gig. I was going to be moving ahead so fast, I'd leave a vapor trail.

Of course, people who own existing concert footage don't just give it away. They want this thing that I was vaguely familiar with called "financial compensation." And then I discovered that the total amount set aside in the budget for these licensing fees would probably have gotten us at best the rights to my brother Marc's wedding video—and definitely not in perpetuity. Yet my task was to fill ten shows' worth of material. Yikes.

But I was determined. And in the process of producing this series, I learned invaluable lessons about raising money for media projects.

Fundraising and preproduction go hand in hand. It is very difficult to begin the latter without the former. You need a plan and an outline before you can try to raise money for your film—a comprehensive presentation that tells the story of who you are and what the project is about, and that gives as much evidence as possible to prove to the world how you're going to make your movie happen—creatively, logistically, and financially.

And the more elements you put together (e.g., actors, a script, a cinematographer), the greater chance you have of raising the funds you need. And even if you want to self-finance, you still need a plan, and making the plan is part of the preproduction process.

True or false: It's never been easier to finance your movie.

You know the answer is "true" without even knowing how you know, right? That, and the fact that I can even pose the question, tells you how dramatically this aspect of the business has shifted. But be warned: Raising money for independent films comes with its own challenges. First, think about what you're asking an investor to do—give you money (often a substantial amount) based on some words written on a page and a vision for where you're going to take those words. There's no way to measure the value of that vision other than by your persuasion and strong conviction. Not exactly a blue-chip investment. And there is no guarantee of a return on the investment.

And trust me, no Nigerian prince you meet online is going to give you the money for your short. (Unless you're Bret or Jemaine from *Flight of the Conchords*, but then again, they had Murray as their manager introducing them to Nigel Soladu. . . . But that's another story.)

Theories of Fundraising

Your most essential sales tool to help raise money for your film project and start your career is your narrative. It is the most important first step you will ever take in this industry.

A narrative, of course, is a story—but the narrative I will write about here is not the narrative of the three-act story of your movie. It is the story about you and your movie: who you are, why this film (short or feature) is unique, why your storytelling angle is unique, and why this project is different from the zillions of other movies out there that people are trying to get made. That narrative needs be a page-turner—amazing, honest, savvy, well prepared, and intelligent—if you want people to agree to back your film. I am not asking you to create a book about your movie, but rather both an oral and written press release/résumé for your movie and you. Tell me, why should I believe in you? What is so interesting and unique about you and your movie? And if you cannot figure that out, then you have to go back to the drawing board until you can.

And the narrative is not just a fundraising tactic. If you remember nothing else, remember this: You are a filmmaker. Act like one. It is your job to step outside yourself and give your project and you an honest assessment of strengths and weaknesses. Knowing this, you can fill in the blanks with as much passion, intelligence, heart, and commitment as you can. By doing so, you define and imbue your project (and yourself) with an energy that will carry you throughout the process, and that will ultimately serve as a powerful starting point for the rest of your career.

You are always selling yourself in this industry, whether you're attempting to persuade an attorney or accountant to work inexpensively, an investor to invest in your film, a writer to write for you, an actor to act for you, or a crew to follow your instructions. All the way through the process—up to and after distribution—it never ends.

Your narrative has to serve you well, and it can . . . if you create it well.

Focus on the positives to create your narrative. But also know your own negatives and be ready to respond to them—the industry is a bit like a bloodhound constantly sniffing out projects and filmmakers for their weaknesses. You're "too in-experienced," you've "never worked in film," you "have no at-tachments," the script is "too long" or "too short" (or "too *anything*"—you'll hear them all). Anticipating the criticism not only helps you prepare for the marketplace but also makes your project stronger. It'll help you solve problems that are fixable and mitigate the ones that are not.

When I first tried putting together my oral and written nar-rative, my pitch on my movie was fine, but I was concerned my general demeanor might not fit into the rough-and-tumble world of filmmaking. We've all heard the Hollywood stories of legendary, cigar-chewing producers and the epic scale of their sharp elbows and volcanic vituperation. I've never been that way and never will be.

But then I discovered something strange: When you pro-mote your project, you don't need to be harsh and loud. In fact, you can even be a little more soft and thoughtful, and still have a career. People want someone and something to believe in. Decision makers feel safe saying no, but there's a tiny part of them that is desperate to say yes. *Yes,* I've found the next big thing. *Yes,* I've got someone who can make it happen. *Yes,* this is a filmmaker with a story to tell and a plan to get there. If your narrative is true and your conviction unshakable, decibel level doesn't matter. At the very least, you're going to walk into any room and meet on an even playing field—all ideas have equal value.

Or as the French dramatist Jean Giraudoux said, "Be who you really are, and if you can fake that, then you really got it made."

Here are some narrative samples:

- Remember that female actor from the Midwest in chapter 4? She was all set to produce and star in a horror movie, which after some reflection didn't make much sense anymore. So she paused, took a step back, assessed who she was, and came up with an idea for her next project, which was a better fit: a small-town girl / fish out of water who comes to the "big city." So now when she starts developing and pitching her film and script, it will be something she knows really well, something that is who she is, and something she really believes in.

- I was approached by a man after one of my seminars who asked me to help him craft his narrative as he went about starting his first short film. He was smart—a clean-cut Wall Street type. However, after talking to him for just a few minutes, I uncovered an interesting fact about his media experience. He was once in a music video that happened to be seen by more than one million people on YouTube. In addition, he is "non-industry" friends with a fairly well-known actor willing to be in his short.

  We then put together his narrative, how he would sell his short and himself to the public: He would start building this specific narrative by finding a short story that best used that actor's strengths. Once he found that short story, he would ask the actor to work with him on it, and then he would write it (or have it written).

Altering his original limp story of a successful finance-industry executive trying to break into the media industry, he created a new narrative that became an overnight sensation, with more than a million views on YouTube, by getting hold of a great script and a prominent actor, and finding smart people to come along for the ride. As this man did, you must discover your most marketable aspects, and then adjust your narrative to focus on those strengths.

I work with Rico Colindres, a very successful Hispanic radio personality. He has been doing radio for many years. He has created and developed specific radio characters during his career. One in particular, Carmen Calls, is his most well known. Rico plays Carmen, a hot-blooded, over-the-top Latina, who calls various real people and then relentlessly, and with a good nature, drives them crazy until they eventually hang up on her.

Rico loves radio but was looking to expand into more visual media markets. And you know what he did? He changed his narrative. Rico was smart enough to know that his Carmen Calls radio bits were funny, but they were simply "bits," like those on the website Funny or Die. He knew he would need more than that in order to expand Carmen into television and film. So he studied television scripts, and began thinking, "I can do that," so he started writing, and went about transforming Carmen from a radio bit into an animated star character of a television series. And along with her transformation came his—he no longer presented himself as just a radio personality but rather as the creator of a television series.

Rico also added to his narrative with a marketing push. His argument went like this: "No one is really serving the burgeoning, assimilating Hispanic television marketplace in America. With my background and established Carmen character, I can do it." Using that angle, he was able to gain the attention of some famous television producers, and together we were able to guide Rico into writing a wonderful *Carmen Calls* television pilot script and marketing approach, which will definitely help launch his career in the television industry. He also now has a wonderful narrative that will stay with him as he moves into the film and television industry.

The amazing thing about these case studies is that the narratives were always there—and I suspect yours is too. It just takes a little thinking to pull them out.

However, I must mention that for every "Gallant" story, there is a matching "Goofus" (a reference to *Highlights for Children* magazine; see Building Block One).

I was working once with a first-time director. I met him and tried to help him create a new narrative. We were able to raise money for him to direct a feature-length film, but there were problems from the get-go—the signs were there.

A friend of mine (and a wonderfully talented cinematographer) named Michael Barrett once said a very smart thing about the film and television industry: There are two types of people who work in this business. The first are those who are in it for the excitement; being involved in entertainment is sexy and thrilling. It's why you can bet even the mailroom and accounting departments at almost every production company are stocked with eager film buffs. The second are the real storytellers. People attracted to the industry as a creative outlet who have the skill and talent to move others with the narratives they weave. Now, while there is nothing wrong with either type, I would much rather be in a foxhole with the second type.

This director clearly belonged to the first type—the one who loved the idea of the industry more than the work itself. As we went about constructing his narrative, he would always begin in reality, but would quickly veer off into a fabulist territory, constructing a version of himself that consisted of narrative elements that had nothing to do with his own personal history. And when this director's narrative fell into this fabulist, storyteller mode (which had nothing to do with his personal strengths), I was always there to remind him that, at this early stage of his new career, this was the wrong area on which to focus. I recounted the "two types" theory to him constantly, and it would always sink in . . . for a short while.

After he completed shooting the film he was working on and was in the final stages of postproduction, I set up meetings in Los Angeles with prominent agents to work towards positioning both the film and his career. And I made sure to coach him one final time before our first meeting.

We then flew to California. I again reminded him of the two types of people who aspire to work in this industry. He listened, but judging by the glazed-over look in his eyes, I was concerned he just wasn't buying it.

We walked into our first meeting with a powerful agent, who asked him to talk about his film. Quickly, my friend jumped up, loudly declaring, "When we become good friends, which I'm sure will happen, you'll know this about me—I'm a natural-born storyteller, and as an artist I talk with my hands, so that's why I am standing." He then proceeded to walk around this large room, grandstanding and pontificating about film, as if he had just directed *Citizen Kane*. It was one of the most embarrassing moments I have ever witnessed in the entertainment industry.

Alas, his "type one" personality couldn't resist coming out, like Peter Sellers's hand giving the Nazi salute in Stanley Kubrick's *Dr. Strangelove*. And when we left the meeting, the agent pulled me aside and commented on the absurdity of this would-be filmmaker. I mentioned it nicely and discreetly to the director afterwards, but he got angry with me and we parted ways.

What should he have done? He should have been very humble, thoughtful, earnest, and passionate about his vision for his film; he should have discussed the types of films he liked and the direction he wanted to go in his future career. He would have then followed up with an e-mail to this agent's office in a week or two, and hopefully a relationship could have been created, and at a minimum, even if the agent did not like his film, this filmmaker would now be on the radar of a well-known agent for future opportunities.

So you can lead a person to his own narrative, but you cannot always make him become it.

These are just a few examples of narratives. The road is both celebrated and littered with them, and you can see now how essential a strong, honest, smart, and passionate one is to breaking into the film and television industry. The bad news is that a negative narrative can ruin your chances of successfully moving forward. The good news is that you can always work on changing your narrative, making it as strong and powerful as you want it to be, regardless of what preceded it. There are always second acts in the entertainment industry.

Practicalities of Fundraising

WARNING: This section can get dense at times, and it calls upon your business muscle more than your creative muscle. So I recommend getting in touch with you inexpensive lawyer or business friend at the appropriate time to go over this material.

Because this is an industry that involves entertaining and the arts, it's easy to lose sight of a simple fact—the financial goal of any film is to "make a return" for your investor. We live in a bottom-line world, and the film and television industry is no different. If your film makes money, you'll probably get a shot to make another one. If your film doesn't make money, the road to film number two becomes longer, twistier, much less well paved, and trickier.

Short Films

With short films, it is really hard to make a financial return. There are always new entities popping up that tell you that you can make your money licensing your short films, but in my personal experience, I have never seen them work out well. It may change sometime in the future, but not right now.

Consequently, I suggest these fundraising ideas for shorts:

- Approach foundations that may have an interest in the subject matter of your film. It is easier if it is a documentary, but you have nothing to lose if you approach a foundation whose specific mandate matches the subject matter of your film.
- Self-finance, or go to family and friends to ask for donations. Since you probably won't make

money on your short, make this a labor of love. You really don't need a vast amount of money to put something together, so find people who believe in you, and let them know the value of what you are doing. There is also section 181 of the federal tax code, which may give them a tax break (to be discussed later in this chapter).

- Create a well-run fundraiser/launch party. For example, have a raffle, live music, whatever you think will make people want to come. Do you have a social friend? One of those people who knows everyone? Perhaps offer them an executive producer credit if they can get fifty people to your launch party. Do you have five social friends? Then you're in business. Also, your key collaborators would be instrumental in bringing people to your fundraiser/launch party.

- Go to a crowdsourcing website. More about this later in this chapter (see page 98).

In addition, almost everybody I've ever met finds the film and television industry extremely glamorous and thrilling. Let your potential investors get involved in the noncreative aspects of the filmmaking process.

For example, entice your investors with an executive or co-executive producer credit. And when you present your overall plan to your potential investor, make it a visual presentation—show them what their credit will look like on the big screen. It will be much more impressive than just saying it. This is a visual medium, so use visuals! Ask them or their family members to have "walk-on" cameos in your film. Ask if any members of their family would like to work on the short. Ask them if they would like you to shoot your short in their house (this one could be a little tricky, but may work under the right conditions).

Although there is little chance that an investor will make his or her money back on a short, there are financial carrots to dangle—such as an indirect return on investors' money. In this case you're asking an investor to take a longer view of the investment. Try pitching along the lines of, "Since you believe in me as I am starting out in my career, and I appreciate that, I can guarantee you a return of your money on any future income I receive on any films and/or television shows I may make." In addition to offering full recoupment to the investor, offer him or her a small percentage of your profits from your next profitable film. This may seem a little too much conjecture for your prospective investor, but it shows a remarkable sense of good faith and fair play on your part, as you want them involved in your life and your successes, because they believed in you from the very beginning.

And always go in fully armed with the following:

1. Your all-important narrative—the story of who you are, what this film is, and why the world needs to see this work.

2. A full complement of schedules showing you have command of the timetables and trajectory of every aspect of the film—preproduction, production, and postproduction, including all possible tax breaks.

3. A well-thought-out marketing, publicity, and distribution plan (using cost-effective social media as your lead). Don't worry: You will have the knowledge and resources to create these elements once you finish reading this book.

Feature Films

Luckily, when it comes to raising money for feature films, there's a marketplace for the product. People want movies. They need movies. Entire industries are based on procuring a pipeline of reliable product. So there are buyers out there.

In addition to the ideas laid out in raising money for short films, historically there have been many ancillary markets after a theatrical run in which to sell your film, thereby enhancing the chances of turning a profit. Markets like pay cable, home video, and foreign sales. However, due to the growth of the Internet, video streaming, and changing end-user licensing plans, these traditional subsidiary markets have dried up for independent films.

But although we've lost a good deal of these ancillary market streams, there has been an explosion of new-market income streams such as video on demand, subscription video on demand, and other online and digital distribution outlets.

We've also gained a remarkable breadth and scope of tax breaks and incentives at both the state and federal level, programs which I will be discussing shortly in this chapter. Specifically, most beginners and many established members of the industry don't even know that, depending on where you shoot, you can have more than half of your budget covered by these kinds of government programs.

But for your sanity, legal protection, and conscience, it is better to underpromise and overperform than the opposite. Make it abundantly clear that this is a highly speculative investment, present your prospective investors with the proper paperwork, and tell them to speak to their lawyer and accountant before they invest in your film.

State Incentives

Many states have created film incentive programs to attract filmmakers, since a film shot in a state has the potential of generating hundreds of thousands of dollars, as well as many jobs. These programs are very effective and are often changing, so do your research to figure out what you actually get in return for shooting in a particular state. For example, do you receive a tax deferment? Do you have to buy discounted tax credits? Are the programs fully funded, i.e., will you actually get money back? And what is the timeline on actually getting your rebate? Some states even have brokers in the middle of the rebate/tax program, who buy your tax credits and then resell them on the marketplace. Film payroll companies like Entertainment Partners and PES are excellent resources to ask questions on the latest various state incentive programs.

After finding a state incentive program you like, I suggest that you then speak with an accountant about your choice. You can find a relatively inexpensive accountant by following the similar ideas I suggested in finding an inexpensive attorney in chapter 2. These include seeking out referrals from nationwide independent-film organizations, college graduate programs in accounting, film-payroll services (such as Entertainment Partners and PES), Craigslist, and employees at your state film commission (who have dealt in depth with low-budget film accountants who apply for their state incentives).

I also suggest that, if possible, you use the state incentives in your home state, even if it may not be the most aggressive program. If not, you may find yourself chasing a big tax break in a state where you don't know anyone. As you're probably doing a low-budget feature, you'll be paying your crew a rate that's inexpensive. But in a state with a great tax incentive, other films will also be in production—many of which will have a bigger budget to pay higher rates for crews. Guess what happens then? Your crew bails for the higher rates and you're the one trying to hold the boom mic and camera at the same time you're directing or acting in a scene, and then you wind up losing your balance, falling over, and cracking a rib, and because you're out of state you have no coverage, and the next thing you know your movie's canceled and you're in a full body cast in a hospital in Juarez, Mexico, and the guy in the hospital bed next to you needs a new kidney and he keeps looking your way (that's the worst case scenario, of course).

And back to the real world, you're now even further behind the eight ball because you're in a state where you have no network to fall back on to replace your crew. And available crew is most likely at a minimum to begin with because this state has so many films being shot there due to its very aggressive incentive program.

You open yourself up to many delays, causing your film, tax incentive and all, to go over budget. I've heard many stories about small productions being derailed exactly that way.

I have used the New York State tax incentive and have found the people behind it to be very responsive and effective. This is particularly impressive, because most of the films shot in New York are higher-budget films; nevertheless, all of the smaller films I have shot in New York have been treated with all the respect and attention of higher-budget projects that I have shot in New York.

New York State has a stand-alone narrative-film postproduction incentive, as well as a full narrative-film production incentive. The postproduction incentive deals with work you have done on the part of your film after you have shot it. So if you shot your film in another state, you can still get a tax rebate for any work you do in completing your film if you do it in New York State. The full narrative-film tax incentive allows you to receive a tax rebate for all the work you have done on your entire film as long as you complete 75 percent of your work in New York State.

Specifically, the New York State full-production program on NYLovesFilm.com reads as follows:

> New York State and New York City's "MADE IN NY" INCENTIVE PROGRAM offers film and television productions that complete 75% of their work in New York State a 30% refundable tax credit from New York State from the budget of below-the-line costs, which include expenses for tangible property or services used in New York directly related to the production (including pre- and postproduction) of the film such as costs of technical and crew production, expenditures for facilities, props, makeup, wardrobe, set construction, and background talent, which will be returned to investors. The credit excludes costs of stories and scripts, and wages for writers, directors, producers and performers (other than extras without spoken lines).

What this clause essentially says is that if you follow these rules, the state of New York will actually give you back a check for 30 percent of all approved below-the-line expenses (they specifically define what approved below-the-line expenses are on their website). And there have not been many events happier for me in my film career than when I end up giving one of those checks back to my investors.

And if you fear that this is too technical for you, be aware that I have found the employees who run these programs in New York State extremely helpful in explaining in simple terms what it is you have to do to walk your way through these rules to get your rebate.

There are specific limitations on who is eligible, and this and all state incentive programs are always changing, so you must check with the individual states and cities online or by phone for the latest updates.

Federal Incentives

The federal government wants filmmakers to shoot in the United States. To avoid having what they call "runaway productions"—that is, films shot outside the United States—they offer two incentives, section 181 and section 199.

Section 199 deals with tax incentives once your film makes a profit, but section 181 has nothing to do with tax incentives for making a profit, but rather with tax incentives just for investing in a film in the United States, and thus it is more immediately important to you. And as uncreative as it sounds, you need to familiarize yourself with section 181 of the American Jobs Creation Act. Because that mouthful of tax-law parlance is a program created by the US government to combat runaway productions outside the United States. It's part of an extensive "tax extenders" bill, created in 2004 and is up for renewal annually, so please check that this tax incentive is still active when shooting your film. At present, section 181 works as follows:

The American Jobs Creation Act of 2004, section 181 of the Internal Revenue Code of 1986, extended on December 17, 2010, dictates that an individual or company who makes an investment into a section 181–qualified production can take a 100 percent deduction of their investment against their passive income in the year their investment was made as long as this tax incentive is still active.

So let's break that down a bit. "Passive" income is income from things like investments—not salary or wages. Get a specific definition from your newly hired accountant. This section states basically that if an individual or corporation has passive income to invest in a film that is section 181–qualified, 100 percent of that investment is tax deductible in the actual year of his or her investment.

If we use some back-of-the-envelope numbers and figure an investment of $500,000 (for example) and assume that would be taxed roughly at a rate of 40 percent (39.6 percent being the highest federal tax rate), the net investment, after specifically applicable and appropriate tax deductions, would end up only being $300,000. See how that works? The investor avoids a tax bill of $200,000 on their $500,000 (40 percent of $500,000 is $200,000). So you can, in a sense, under the right circumstances (with specific advice from your accountant), promise your investor he's going to pay $200,000 less in passive income taxes that year because of investing in your film. Guaranteed. By Uncle Sam.

These programs are complex, constantly changing, and may sound too "wonky" for some, but remember, you now have an inexpensive accountant and lawyer working with you who can help. And if not, you can suggest to your prospective investor that he asks his accountant if he fits into this program.

If you make a film in New York State, you get back a check from New York State for 30 percent of all your below-the-line costs (let's say that translates into 20 percent of your entire budget), and if your investor is able to take the full 40 percent tax write-off in the same year, on a $500,000 film, the investor, blending both programs, would get back a check for $100,000 from New York State and a federal tax deduction from the IRS for $200,000, equaling 60 percent of the investor's investment.

It is exciting to know that they will get these incentives even if the film is never shown anywhere. These incentives are dependent upon spending money on film, not making money on film.

And whether you are raising money for a short film or a feature narrative film, try *not* to raise partial film financing and then start your movie. Stories of shooting a film without having all of your money in place often don't end well. So you should put together a tight budget, and go forward with it (regarding how to make this budget, you will need a line producer, something I discuss in chapter 6).

Your Worth as a Filmmaker

When you put together your budget, you may consider paying yourself a fee for your first film. And furthermore, if you stick to the plan I'm laying out, you will hopefully one day be in a position to make an arrangement for your services as a filmmaker. Thus you might be wondering: What is the fair-market value of my filmmaking services, and what is the money worth in terms of helping get my career started?

As an attorney representing hundreds of clients over the years, I have some very specific and strong opinions on this subject. What is someone worth, in cold financial terms, when he or she is just starting out in the industry?

Nothing. Yes, nothing.

It might sound harsh, but try to remember: New filmmakers should be happy to get a chance to show their skills, to get an opportunity to produce something real and come away with a showpiece that broadcasts to the industry what he or she can do, if given the chance. Of course you have some worth, but you have to be flexible in your negotiations and expectations. If you have talent (and have followed the principles in this book), when you do "arrive," you can command whatever salary the marketplace will bear on your next project. Talent is talent; it always rises to the top. The challenge, even for the most skilled filmmakers out there, is how to make a film and get it seen in order to get "on the boards" and jump-start your career.

I don't like to disparage one of the professions of which I'm a member, but the real problem in negotiating some of these first-time agreements for a filmmaker's services often comes down to lawyers and agents. Here's something you have to keep in mind: Often, lawyers make money by *extending* the negotiations, not necessarily by closing deals. I've seen numerous situations where attorneys and agents find that the best way to keep their clients paying them is to appeal to their sense of fear and insecurity.

This issue has become particularly acute for talent in the last few years because of Building Block Two (New-Media Technology—Equipment). Many, many more people can afford media equipment—with applications like GarageBand, iMovie, Final Cut Pro, Audio Protools, Adobe After Effects, Adobe Photoshop, and iDraw. Access to the tools you need for a media career has never been easier. So with these traditional barriers eliminated, many more people have the chance to prove themselves in the industry. Inexperienced people in small towns who would have never before had the access to the media tools or the opportunity to show their work now have the chance to let their talent compete in the marketplace, and market themselves as aggressively as the new media allows (Building Block Three).

Of course all lawyers and agents aren't deliberately slow-walking their clients' careers in order to enrich themselves. And you won't always encounter attorneys and agents who stall to close deals. I've dealt with phenomenal talent agents and lawyers who represent their clients with class and foresight. But remember: When the time comes to negotiate a deal, pay very close attention to whose interest your agent or lawyer is looking out for, because it may not be 100 percent yours.

Three "worthy" cases in point:

1. When looking for a music composer for a low-budget film I recently produced, *One Fall*, I interviewed an up-and-coming composer. The composer sent me a sample thirty-second "mini-composition" that he saw as the musical spine for the film. I heard it, liked it very much, and we decided to hire him. Recognizing that this was a great opportunity for him to get his work out there, he quickly agreed to our terms.

   Now keep in mind, there are thousands of musicians and aspiring composers just hoping for the chance to score a feature film. You'd think a deal like this would be easy to close. It's not.

   At the last minute, the composer's agent decided to make more demands than we had agreed to when we originally made our deal. Because the composer suddenly felt he was not getting enough money for his work on our low-budget film, his agent began demanding that her client retain the copyright to that thirty-second sample composition. I told her this music sample was the very reason why we hired him, and that the film's music would be based on this musical motif. It wouldn't make sense to let the composer own the copyright, as he could then use it for any other project he wanted—even one that competed with our film!

   I even offered her the option to have the mini-composition revert back to the composer a few years after the film was released, but she would not budge.

The final outcome?

We found someone else, Ben Toth, a very talented composer with whom we negotiated a reasonable agreement. He did a really great job, and has since had a terrific career in film and theater.

The original composer?

He's doing exactly the same thing he was before he and his agent decided they should hold out for a better deal and not score the film: translating to nothing.

2. Such situations aren't limited to just lower-budget films. I was once producing a film with a higher budget, where the director found an obscure music composer in the Midwest—a librarian by day and a music composer on the side. The director really liked his music and wanted to give him his big break.

    Since it was a bigger-budgeted film, we were able to pay him a decent fee. He was thrilled. And then he hired an entertainment lawyer in New York to negotiate the entire contract. The first thing the attorney did was double the fee we offered his client. We told him that this was our final offer, and that we were giving his client a once-in-a-lifetime opportunity. But it soon became clear that it was more about the attorney's ego than his client's opportunities. He passed on behalf of his client. We went to someone else, who did a very good job.

    The original musician? It's been quite a few years, but last time I heard, he was still a librarian in the Midwest.

3. I was recently working with a first-time filmmaker. This filmmaker had an old college friend who was now interested in financing his first film. Against my advice, he put together a budget in which he would be getting a significant salary. He told me not to be concerned, that this was an old dear friend of his, and his salary wouldn't be a problem.

    The outcome?

    Such was not the case; the friend was incensed, and the film was never made.

So don't be greedy about what you're worth—particularly when you're first starting out. Entertainment is a hypercompetitive, unforgiving industry. While it's important to advocate on your own behalf, a great opportunity is much more valuable than a great payday at the beginning. Fears of getting taken advantage of have led many to become overly cautious, and to not take chances. Always weigh the benefits and liabilities of each situation, and make a nonemotional decision based upon what you feel will best move you career forward. I promise you: The answer isn't always to make the most money possible.

However, there are certain circumstances where just the opposite may be true. I was representing a young, talented writer who owned a prominent, highly desired, trademarked asset. He was approached by a well-known talent in the industry who wanted to work with him and his particular asset. But the terms were totally weighed in favor of the well-known talent. The argument he made was that my client was still young, whereas he was successful, so my client should therefore take a second position to him in the exploitation of my client's asset.

My client grew up watching the well-known talent's programs, and was willing to give up control of his project to the talent.

I did some research on this well-known talent on IMDbPro, and it turned out that although he was at one time very successful, he hadn't had a success in years and was recently fired from his last two projects. I brought this information to my client in the hopes of persuading him to ask for a more equitable arrangement with the well-known talent. I was told to ask for a more equitable split, and when I did, the well-known client started screaming and threatened to leave the project.

I was sure that this well-known talent wasn't going to leave the project (he had nowhere else to go), but my client was fearful and did not listen to me, and signed the inequitable deal.

The outcome?

A few years have passed and the project is still languishing in an inequitable arrangement, while going nowhere.

So weigh every potential arrangement from both sides, knowing what you have to offer and its real value, versus what value is on the other side of the table in terms of future possibilities of success for you.

Crowdsourcing/Crowdfunding

Crowdsourcing and *crowdfunding* are the new buzzwords that refer to raising money for your media projects online. It refers to the proliferation of websites and new-media channels that bring together potential backers and potential projects. The theory goes that the web gives you access to thousands (if not millions) of potential donors, and if you can get a crowd of them to chip in a small amount each, you can get thousands to millions of dollars for a production. It's an intriguing angle.

At present, Kickstarter is the most prominent site for filmmakers. It is an unregulated donation model where people list their creative projects online (at any stage along the project's development, from initiation to final distribution) and ask for funding for those projects from the public, usually in exchange for a gift of some sort. Most significantly, the financial contributors do not receive equity for their donation.

But please speak to your attorney and/or tax accountant about the ramifications of receiving money for your film. As attractive as this option can seem, there are some very tricky legal situations that never occur to filmmakers until they are hit with a big tax problem when the film is completed.

To make things even more interesting in this area, up until recently, United States securities laws prohibited the purchase of securities without following particular laws. Consequently, crowdsourcing sites like Kickstarter could only legally give the person donating the money a "gift," but not an actual piece of the project. However, on April 5, 2012, the JOBS Act was passed into law, which now opens up equity crowdsourcing/funding for projects up to $1 million. They are still working out the particulars with the Securities and Exchange Commission, but once this is completed, offering equity for an investment, as opposed to a mere small gift for a donation, could open the floodgates for investing in independent film.

In the past you could only submit film *investment* opportunities to individuals, and weren't able to advertise them to the masses (including crowdfunding sites). But now, because of Title II of the JOBS Act, you may be able to crowdfund online with certain limitations to approximately nine million US accredited investors (an accredited investor is defined as an individual or couple with a net worth of more than $1 million, excluding their primary residence, or an individual with an income exceeding $200,000 in the two most recent years, or $300,000 for a couple). And as per Title III of the JOBS Act, you may be able to advertise to unaccredited investors, with certain restrictions soon to be determined by the Securities and Exchange Commission.

And traditional crowdfunding websites are flocking to use the JOBS Act, with some like Indiegogo teaming up with industry stalwart *Backstage* magazine, all lining up film projects and/or investors. Jason Best, cofounder of Crowdfund Capital Advisors, estimates that the equity crowdfunding market could reach $4 billion in four years, with a significant portion of that going to filmmakers. Independent filmmaking has the opportunity for the first time in its history to be on an even playing field with entrepreneurs and accredited film-loving investors, both by online crowdfunding and by approaching investors directly.

Obviously this kind of fundraising has the potential to be a major, powerful tool for a beginning filmmaker—*Slate* called it a "fundraising game-changer." But here too, we are at the beginning of another new-media concept, and most people don't know how to maximize their chances for raising money on these sites, or how to take advantage of the new benefits in the JOBS Act.

Because it has such a low barrier of entry (i.e., anyone with a computer and a film project can do it), it once again becomes that much harder to stand out from the masses that are now crowding your sources.

By the time you finish reading this book, you'll be an expert at knowing how to sell your project. That expertise can be put to good use on your crowdfunding web page, and in general to reach that new pool of potential film investors. You need to distinguish yourself from every other project out there—creatively, graphically, financially, logistically, and from a marketing and distribution standpoint—in every conceivable way. Just because your project will be low budget, it doesn't mean you can't present yourself in a high-end way.

Your online sales package (that can be used offline too,

when presenting to individual accredited investors) that repre-
sents your film in its very best light should include the following
elements:

- compelling and attractive graphics introducing the
  project
- your narrative, and the narrative of your project
- the best possible description of your work, and
  if you have any footage already shot, pictures, or
  talent attached. Kickstarter's research has shown
  that adding a video to your presentation increases
  your chances of success by 20 percent
- references, testimonials
- a marketing, publicity, and distribution plan (to be
  discussed in chapters 9 and 10)
- links to your previous work if you have them, or
  the work itself, if appropriate
- links to as many related and responsible entities
  that you can
- a creative, equitable, interesting, and compelling
  gift in exhange for their donation, or in the case
  of JOBS Act investments, an equitable profit-
  participation structure for your investors

Be realistic with what you are asking for financially, and
what it covers. It may make sense to go piecemeal by raising
small portions of money for different sections of your project
on these sites. Recent data have shown that the more modest
your financial requests are, the greater your chances are of finding sympathetic backers while crowdsourcing. I am not a big
proponent of raising money piecemeal, but if you go the piecemeal route, your investors should know the risks with that
approach.

Once your sales package is complete and you are online, you've only just started. You have to now aggressively get the word out about your project and its needs. At this stage it becomes a numbers game—the more eyeballs there are to see your presentation, the greater your chances are of receiving donations. Get in touch with all your friends and associates, and use film- and television-based social-media networks (there are so many of them out there).

Also, remember to always be mindful of the rules and regulations of the various crowdsourcing/funding sites—they are quite different for each site (some let you keep any money you raise, and for some it's all or nothing).

Crowdsourcing/crowdfunding may represent great new tools for aspiring filmmakers. But you can't be lax or naïve about how you use it. Otherwise you'll end up as background noise with the other zillion wannabes with their hands out, hoping for a break. Do the work.

And how did my first media-fundraising experience turn out for my rock-and-roll summer series, because someone in a steam room mistook me for an actual producer? I succeeded. Sort of.

> I started calling everyone I knew who was even tangentially related to the music industry (relatives, college roommates, anyone) who could introduce me to people who owned music footage. And the funny thing is, if you are actually offering to pay someone for material to air on nationwide television, it is amazing how quickly your network grows. So in the best "six degrees of separation" sequence, within weeks I had met tons of people who had product to license to me. The issue then became how little I had to offer them to license their concert footage.

And after much begging, cajoling, convincing, and persuading, I filled up all ten slots with footage from well-known people like Don Kirshner and Dick Clark. These guys were titans of the entertainment world. The footage was approved and signed off by my ad exec. It was an incredible challenge, but I had succeeded and had ended up coming in under my ultralow budget, primarily because that footage I was obtaining licenses for had already had its primary airing, so this was found money for these licensors. I couldn't wait for the hard work to pay off.

But when it came time to pay these icons of the business—people I had spent months with in a high-wire act of back-and-forth negotiations—all of a sudden my ad exec stopped returning my calls. So I kept calling. And calling. And calling. And he never called me back.

Eventually I got to the bottom of what happened by speaking to a colleague of the ad exec, who I had gotten to know while obtaining the footage. It turned out that the ad exec thought his sponsor client would approve going forward with the summer series without the prominent hosts that they had in the past summers. But at the last moment, his sponsor changed his mind—and decided to pull the plug on the entire show. No prominent hosts. No summer series. No production. No fees. No producer credit for me. And no need for the footage I'd spent months acquiring. Footage that was owned by licensors who were expecting to be paid. And my licensing contracts stated that I had to pay them within fourteen days of execution of the agreements, a time that was now upon me.

My legal-collections business for the Queens dentist was suddenly looking better and better. I had done nothing illegal (thank goodness for my language in the contracts I drafted), but nonetheless, I had a lot of explaining to do. I went to Dick Clark first, because he had been a total pleasure to deal with throughout the negotiations. I took a deep breath and told him the story. There was a long silence when I finished explaining what had happened. I don't remember the exact words he said to me when he finally did speak, but I'll remember the lesson I learned from him forever.

He said that because I had been so straight with him during our negotiations, so sincere and decent to deal with, he—and everybody else—would understand. It would be okay. He would personally make sure of it.

And that attitude, that act of kindness, goes a long way for me in overcoming some of the "valleys" I encounter in the industry. Dick Clark called the others as a courtesy to me, and let them know he would be forgiving and understanding of my situation, and they should be as well. And that everything would be fine. And he did. And it was.

So I didn't produce the series, I didn't get a credit for my résumé, and it didn't propel me to my next success. But I did learn a great deal about being hardworking, a little less naive, straightforward, and passionate about what you do in life.

After all was said and done, it was a much more valuable experience than just producing my first show.

So at this point you should be asking yourself, "What happens next, now that I've raised the funds for my film?"

PREPRODUCTION

The Best-Laid Plans

Things were coming together for my directorial debut. I was excited—alternately confident and scared to death that I would instantly forget everything I'd ever known about filmmaking the moment I showed up on set. It was a heady time.

While in preproduction, much like every other film director without deep pockets and on a short deadline, I had to make a lot of decisions very quickly: picking locations, choosing a cast, and, of course, crewing up. Sometimes, particularly on low-budget films, making quick decisions can be liberating. You don't have time to agonize and belabor every move. And I did make my share of great choices—both logistically and creatively. Sometimes, though, the faster you act, the easier it is to get tripped up.

We had hired a first assistant director for our film. Now, for those of you who don't know, a first assistant director (or first AD) is very different from an assistant "to" a director. The first AD manages time, logis-

tics, coordination, and communication on a set. He or she assists the director in making decisions about what to shoot that day and when to shoot it, all the while ensuring that every moving part of a film is in sync. It's a hugely important position. And ours wasn't working out.

In the frenetic days of low-budget preproduction, I did not have adequate time to do a full reference check on the person I hired to be my first AD. He had done many movies, been trained by a successful first AD, and talked a very good game. But it wasn't long before he, and the crew he brought along with him, started not working out.

I learned firsthand how a weak first AD can cost you time and money, and even how it can cause you to commit a cardinal sin of filmmaking—causing a scene to be cut, not for creative reasons, but because of mismanaged production. From day one, the film started suffering. Badly.

It's a little insane to fire a first assistant director in the middle of shooting a low-budget film. They know things about your project that no one else on the set knows. It's like firing the foreman.

But we had no choice. It was my opinion that his lack of skill and negative attitude were causing major problems, both creatively and financially. So on Friday afternoon we asked him to leave, and he and his crew (about six additional people) took off. This was a huge step off a very high ledge—Marlen and I had made some replacement inquiries, but had no idea if we would find anyone to fill the void.

You can't even get through a single day of production on a full movie set without an AD team. If we couldn't *find replacements within the next twenty-four to forty-eight hours, we would probably have to shut down our film. My hopes and dreams for the success of my directorial debut were quickly in jeopardy.*

My script was ready, the actors were prepared, the money was in place, everything ready to go—but due to a lack of adequate preproduction hiring skills on my part, everything was quickly falling apart.

Without a split second's worry, Marlen took to the phones, calling everyone she knew, trying to find us a first assistant director and an entire department before time ran out . . . in less than two days. And after the first day, we still had no real leads. . . .

Okay, so now back to you. It's your turn—you're in preproduction of your first film, and now everything is real.

You've got a script, and you're putting together your entire package. Take a deep breath and congratulate yourself. All too often we go so fast that we never stop to smell the roses, or enjoy the mini-victories we get on the road to our goal.

But don't pause too long. If you've got good material, the best thing you can do for yourself and your career is to put a marker down and start planning your shoot.

There are major issues to deal with along every step of the filmmaking process—obstacles and challenges that can sink your film, or take you to transcendent places. Fortunately, most of the problems can be avoided or allayed by having a smart, well-planned "preproduction" schedule. This is a crucial segment of the entire process—when the rarefied aspirations of a script and your vision finally begin to become concrete.

First question: What's your mind-set like when starting your first film? Now, every book on directing speaks on how important it is to multitask—that is, that filmmakers benefit from the ability to do many things well at virtually the same time. While this is true to an extent, the word *multitasking* creates a myth. We can't *really* do two things at the same time; instead, we rapidly shift from one to the other, and then back again. Often this translates to not devoting enough attention to any one job, and consequently we end up sacrificing the quality of our attention.

What to do? A multitude of recent studies shows that the simple technique of "mindfulness" is extraordinarily helpful in multitasking, and this is particularly useful for filmmakers. Mindfulness is a daily meditation-like exercise of concentration—the ability to quiet one's mind and focus on the present only, dissolving all distractions. This simple daily practice only takes a few minutes a day, and it has shown to have remarkable success in teaching people to become more aware of their surroundings, as well as how to better concentrate on the many things that may be going on around them. Just go to a place where you can be alone, close your eyes, breathe deeply for anywhere from ten to thirty minutes, and then go back to your film. As a filmmaker, this can be an invaluable exercise.

So now that you have the proper mind-set, you are ready to begin.

Starting Your Film

The first step in the preproduction stage is to create your company vehicle (e.g., an LLC or a corporation) the moment you have an asset that needs protecting. You can go online to find corporate-legal-services companies (such as BlumbergExcelsior Corporate Services) that can assist you in this process. For once you start your film, you are presenting yourself to the public, and issues like copyright and employment will present themselves to you. You are now running a company that is making a film, and you should seek out all the protections the legal system can provide you. It is not that expensive, and you might want to speak to that inexpensive lawyer to get a general sense of things. As you begin this journey, this early step can also save you many problems in the long run.

Hiring your crew and actors as well as planning the shoot are primarily what preproduction is all about. When you put together a film (feature or short), you are creating a fully functioning corporation or LLC with assets, employees, and profits. As a start-up company, you are immediately up and running.

In the preproduction phase, the way you search for and hire your film's essential crew members should follow a very specific and crucial strategy. Done wrong, it can be disastrous (recall the disaster story with my AD). Done right, it can seem like a miracle.

Part One: Hiring

Theories of Hiring

Hiring crew personnel is so important, yet it is often not given enough attention. It's easy to understand why—the connection between your film's success and its cast is much easier to see than, say, the connection between the film and its script supervisor. Or its production secretary. Or its makeup artist. Or its location manager. Nevertheless, always remind yourself that *every* position is vital, and that, although we may be creating art and/or entertainment, we are doing it within the confines of a daily working, functional company. Hiring is an art and should be treated as such.

Nobel Prize–winning economist Daniel Kahneman is a strong proponent of thoughtful hiring. He specifically suggests in his book, *Thinking, Fast and Slow*, to:

- select six traits that are prerequisites for the specific position you are looking to fill (e.g., technical proficiency, good personality, responsibility);
- make a list of questions for each trait, with a sliding scale of one to five (five being the best);
- meet the candidate, and then score him or her from one to five on each of these six traits, scoring the traits one at a time, without skipping around; and
- choose the candidate who had the highest overall score in your ratings system, regardless of whether you liked this person the best.

Although this is a thoughtful and impressive rubric, I wouldn't be too slavish to formulas, especially when it comes to something as imperfect as judging job candidates. But organizing your thoughts about potential hires in this manner can be an invaluable part of your process.

For instance, if you know that responsibility is an indispensable trait for the specific position you are looking for, look to how the candidate responds to deadlines and instructions. If you ask the candidate to call you back between two-thirty and three p.m., was that done? Does the candidate provide you the names and contact numbers of his or her references as promised during the interview? These small tasks speak resoundingly of candidates' skill sets and personalities.

And don't forget to dig deep into credentials. I remember once interviewing a production designer. She had a very strong portfolio and seemed like a nice person. After we reviewed her application, I asked to see some information supporting her portfolio. She suddenly became very indignant, saying that she had never been asked that before in all of her years of being interviewed. Rather than taking offense, I thanked her for the compliment and then asked her for her references—I took it to mean I was the most thorough, thoughtful interviewer she had ever encountered.

Needless to say we did not hire her, but I was curious and went a little further. Some poking around revealed that this designer's assistant had been doing the heavy lifting over the more recent years for her. Perhaps this particular designer got so indignant because her assistant had recently gone out on her own, leaving her as a disaster waiting to happen. Something as simple as asking for backup information supporting a candidate's résumé can initiate some red flags, and turn out to be the difference between a good hiring decision and a potentially calamitous one.

Checking your candidate's references is another imperative part of the hiring process. You can tell a lot about a person by the people they choose to have vouch for them. One of the main reasons I wanted to see backup and references from that production designer candidate was her hesitation to provide any recent references. That set off a bit of a red flag, so I wanted to know more.

And if references do not call you back, mention that to your candidate, and ask him or her to urge their references to get in touch. If you still don't hear anything, you should pay close attention to what that's telling you (or not telling you).

On the positive side, when I was looking for a cinematographer on my directorial debut, I knew how crucial this hire would be for me, particularly with my lack of knowledge in this area. Marlen and I spent hours and hours searching, but could not come up with anyone available whom we liked. With time running out, we called all the film schools in our area, and got demo reels of film school students and graduate students. None of them were very impressive, but then one reel really stood out, that of Michael Barrett—we saw about six shorts he shot, and his work was just brilliant.

We checked him out further, and he turned out to be a teaching graduate assistant. We were very concerned as to why someone this good after shooting six shorts was still a graduate assistant. We called a few of the directors he had worked with, and they all raved about him. I then asked one why he was still a teaching graduate assistant. She said, "Just meet him. You won't regret it."

We met him, and the mystery was solved. When he walked into the room we saw a shy, *very* youthful looking, unassuming student. So much of our industry is surface-oriented, and I could imagine people looking at him and not seeing "confidence." But his reel was great, his references were sterling, he was extremely knowledgeable, and we all got along very well. So we took a risk, and hired a graduate assistant for the most important position on our film.

And it worked out amazingly. He brought a crew that was talented and loyal, one that was more than willing to work the long hours needed in a low-budget film. And Michael's taste was wonderful, and his knowledge bailed us out of quite a few jams.

And since then Michael has gone on to be one of the foremost cinematographers in the country, shooting such films as *Bobby, Kiss Kiss Bang Bang, You Don't Mess with the Zohan, Bedtime Stories, Ted, A Million Ways to Die in the West,* and many, many more.

And as you continue to march into the new-media environment, take advantage of its assets: Ask any candidate you are seriously interested in for them to "friend" you on Facebook. You need to tap every advantage you can, and online profiles like this can tell you a lot about the person you may want to hire. At first blush this may seem like strange advice, but it's extremely effective, and is now being used in many large corporations' human-resources departments.

Not everyone is going to be forthcoming with references, backup, or with social media. This shouldn't necessarily rule someone out as a hire, but the way people respond to information requests can be a useful criterion for evaluating those who will go on to comprise your crew.

When you are making a film, you are literally running a company, and what may seem like obvious tenets of good business (such as hiring personnel) somehow go out the window. Without exaggeration I would say that more than 50 percent of the time I check references, I am told by the referent that they have never been called to check references on this person. It is as if once you decide to make a film, all common business sense disappears. So pay attention by looking at this chapter as a sound and fundamental training manual for things you should be aware of—working in art does not give you license to lose sound business sense.

Practicalities of Hiring

While there are many in-depth guides written on the array of film jobs that exist in the industry (see Sidney Lumet's *Making Movies*), for our purposes I will focus on seven crucial crew positions—the line producer, the cinematographer, the special-effects director, the music composer, the editor, the casting director, and the actors.

I've worked with plenty of directors. Great ones, first-timers, mediocre ones, and some not-so-good ones. And the one thing that holds true, for every director, at any level of talent or experience, is this: If you have a very strong script, wonderful visuals, great music, a very talented cinematographer, and terrific actors, the direction will almost always be good. I am overstating the case somewhat, but if all these elements are locked down creatively, the film, in a funny way, starts to direct itself.

Now, as we're talking primarily about low-budget projects, you may need to persuade many of these hires into volunteering their services for your first film. Why would they do this? If you have a strong enough narrative, you can get your crew to really believe in your film. Especially if they are just starting out in the industry, a certain artistic kinship can form, complete with strong bonds and communality of goals.

Where do you find these prospective candidates?

1. **Word of mouth:** I cannot overemphasize how important this is. Get recommendations from people you respect. It is both the easiest route to take and the one with the greatest chance of success. After that, work "down the line," asking friends to ask their friends, who could then ask their friends, and see where it takes you.

2. **Film schools:** Go to any nearby film schools and post a bulletin. With a strong narrative, you never know what you can come up with.

3. **Building Block One:** There are hundreds of websites that have thousands of people interested in working with start-up filmmakers. I have read the blogs of some amazing high school student filmmakers who clearly have a remarkable understanding of the filmmaking process. With the Internet, this is not your grandparents' low-budget movie world anymore.

4. **Building Block One (part two):** Spend the extra few dollars and subscribe to the bible of filmmaking: IMDbPro. By becoming a subscriber to IMDbPro,

you gain fingertip access to thousands of prospective employees and collaborators. It's like having a filmmaker's almanac—addresses and track records for every position in the industry. It is probably one of the most invaluable resources you can have right now in the filmmaking process.

5. **Serendipity and counterintuitive thinking:** By being out there and keeping your eyes and ears wide open, you never know what you can find. For our first film, *Spanking the Monkey,* we found our lead actor, the future Emmy winner Jeremy Davies, by seeing him on a Subaru television commercial. Although the commercial was only thirty seconds, he kept our attention, so crucial in choosing a lead for your film. So from that brief glance, we met him, auditioned him, and cast him.

The Team

Now that you know where to find the people who will work on your film, here are the key positions you'll need to fill on your first film set.

Line Producer

I've often mused that the term "line" producer denotes the fact that the person filling this role always has his or her "you know what" on the line. This is your workhorse—the engine of the production. Everything runs through the line producer: Insurance. Catering. Human resources. Contracts. Security. Scheduling. Making the film's budget. Overseeing hiring, firing. He or she is like a "sergeant at arms," accountable for the daily running of the company that is making the film, and responsible for the film finishing on budget and on time. You cannot make a move without your line producer and it should be your first company hire.

Experience is very important, but so too are intelligence, passion, and drive. The line producer on *Spanking the Monkey* (which was so low budget that everyone would only be paid speculatively in any future profits) had never done the job before in his life, but he was smart, learned quickly, and ended up performing well.

I have found that state film commission representatives, who are in the business of soliciting filmmakers to shoot in their state, are very helpful in recommending line producers, due to their experience working with them firsthand (line producers have to file extensive reports with the state film commissions in order to get tax rebates on their films).

But beware: I have been shocked to discover how few line producers have any expertise in postproduction. Too often their feeling is that their job ends when the production finishes shooting, which is incredibly shortsighted. It's akin to saying: "Here are the ingredients for the cake you are baking. I'm happy to help you make sure each ingredient is fresh and ready, help you mix the ingredients in the right order, sift the flour, and crack the eggs—I'll even preheat your oven. But I'm not going to stick around to see if I made any mistakes when the cake comes out of the oven. And I don't really care how it tastes."

Some productions can afford a "postproduction supervisor," or someone who basically serves as the line producer through postproduction—that is, after the film is finished with the day-to-day process of shooting. However, especially on a small film, it's imperative that you find a line producer with some experience working on a film in its final stages. That knowledge will help you determine how the postproduction work flow (which begins while you're shooting) is budgeted, while allowing you to anticipate and solve many of your post-production problems even before they happen.

Cinematographer

As far as the look and movement of a film goes, there is practically no more important person on a set than the cinematographer. Working with the director, the cinematographer will help define the look and feel of your film. And defining those things involves a continuous set of creative decisions: What camera should you use? Should you shoot in digital or in film? Should you aim for smooth, linear shots, or a more naturalistic look using a handheld portable camera, as opposed to a stationary camera? Should the visual tones be saturated? Dark? Should the look be crisp and clean or romantic and a little softer? What will the shot list (a list cinematographers make ahead of time that outlines the shots they anticipate taking during each scene) look like?

In addition to helping define the visual style of your film, your cinematographer is a little like a creative consigliere, helping you figure out how to shoot action scenes, how to shoot sequences, how to determine what material will cut together well—even assisting in managing your time and consolidating shots to help make sure you get everything you need.

Also, make sure that your cinematographer knows about the editing process—the good ones always do. These skills will allow him or her to get material that will edit together well, making your life so much easier during the editing process.

Furthermore, make sure your cinematographer knows digital if that's the format you've chosen to work in. He or she will likely know more than you, but you can tell a lot by how a cinematographer answers questions about the differences between lighting for film and for digital (more on digital in chapter 7), and by how they feel about different lenses that they will use with their camera. This is crucial; the right lens can make all the difference in the world in elevating the quality of your film. And look up technical stats on IMDbPro on films that have a look and feel you like. That way, the cinematographer and you can get a sense of the camera and lenses that you may want to use. Also, research your cinematographer's camera, if he or she has one, and find out its particular strengths and weaknesses.

If you have a cinematographer who talks more about how beautiful he or she will make each scene than about any of the specifics, run as fast as you can in the other direction and find someone more experienced with the particulars of shooting a movie.

I have had a lot of luck finding cinematographers by poring over hundreds and hundreds of student films (you can find them through Building Block One). It is a lot of hard work, but when you discover that one diamond in the rough, it will all have been worth it. Because the person looking through the eyepiece of the camera is your first and best creative collaborator in defining every visual aspect of your movie.

Special-Effects Director

When considering the role of your special-effects director, recall the earlier chapters where I discussed the importance of distinguishing yourself from the legion of competitors out there. Whether you start out with the genres I've suggested (comedy or science fiction) or not, it's always important to remember Building Block Two (New-Media Technology—Equipment) as you consider ways to make your work stand out.

A primary way of doing this could be to take advantage of

special effects, which are less expensive and easier to use than ever and can add a patina of professionalism and production value that really makes your movie pop. Even if you do not make a science fiction film, I urge you to find creative ways to use special effects—and special effects can be as minimal as changing the sign on a store, or as major as making an explosion. But at the same time, please remember to use special effects only if it's organic to the story. The worst choice you can make is to employ special effects that have nothing to do with your film—it's a dishonest choice that will be quickly apparent to your viewers.

It is also important to bring the special-effects director on board in preproduction—do not wait until after filming. Though counterintuitive, the most important part of the special-effects director's job actually happens *before* you shoot anything. Special-effects shots always take extra planning. Information about camera position, landscape, background, foreground, and camera movement will impact the scope and cost of your effects work. So being meticulous about setting up all the special-effects shots ahead of time is not only critical in getting the best-quality work, but can also save you money in the execution of those effects.

You might feel that setting out to find someone in such a skilled field who is both inexpensive and supremely talented is a fool's errand. Thankfully, though, it's really no different from finding any other position (film shorts, film schools, Kickstarter, websites, IMDbPro, etc.)—all made possible because of the creation of a new and growing community of collaborative professionals due to Building Block Two.

We found one of our most recent special-effects hires by watching his student film. He ended up doing an amazing job, and at a very cost-effective price as well.

Music Composer

People who don't really know filmmaking always underestimate the importance of sound, and the monumental storytelling craft needed in scoring a movie. I've seen a film's marketing percentages shoot from middling to miraculous without one change to a significant frame of footage. Simply changing the music—often a film's emotional guide—can completely reshape a viewer's experience of a story.

All too often the filmmaker waits until the film is over to look for a music composer. But why wait? If you can find someone to score your film during preproduction, you will be far ahead of the game, and the final product will clearly reflect the extra time that went into it.

So where do you find your composer? Same game, new rules (Building Block One). In addition to recommendations, the Internet, film school shorts, and shorts in general, check out the music theaters in your area and listen to the scores; if you like what you hear, try to get in touch with that composer or band directly. Everyone wants to get into the film industry, so your chances are strong that whomever you find will be eager to work with you—and for not a lot of money.

Editor

I have had the privilege and good fortune to work with editor Hughes Winborne on *The Last Good Time,* who later went on to win an Oscar for editing *Crash.*

Hughes had a rough cut of our film, an original mass of wonderful scenes, and he was able to work with director Bob Balaban to make sense of it all. We ended up with an amazing film. That is the value of a strong, talented editor.

You can find good editors using the suggestions I make in

this chapter. But because of the direct aesthetic intimacy and the months and months of time you will spend with your editor dissecting your film—more alone time than with any other person during your film's life cycle—it is imperative that you interview prospective editors much more thoroughly than you do any other position.

Often, because the editor is usually one of the last hires you make, you don't pay as much attention to it as you had done for your previous hires, which is a huge mistake. I have experienced films where editors get along wonderfully with directors, and other films where I had to actually stop physical altercations (including throwing lamps!) between a director and editor.

Casting Director

Not everyone can spot poor lighting in a movie. Or a movie that has poor art direction, or was poorly scored, or edited, or even written. But *everyone* can spot a movie that's poorly acted.

Casting is a remarkable art, one I did not fully appreciate until after I was forced to use a casting director. Virtually everyone, myself included, who loves film feels that they know actors. How could they not? So when I started out, we had very little money for our film, so the thinking was, why bother hiring a casting director? My friends and I, major aficionados of film, knew all the good actors. But I quickly realized that I was wrong.

As much as I felt I knew actors, casting directors always knew more, were more objective, and could give me insights at every step of the casting process that someone outside the acting world could never know. As much as I thought my friends and I knew, it was not close to what I would need to know. Casting directors don't just know well-known actors; it is their job to find the *next generation* of well-known actors, or actors we don't know of who have slipped through the cracks—something essential for a low-budget film.

An example of the increasing industry awareness of the importance of casting directors is the recent decision by the Academy of Motion Picture Arts and Sciences (AMPAS) regarding casting directors. AMPAS, an organization comprised of fewer than five thousand members, of which I am one, decides on the Oscars, and just recently we decided to create an actual branch for casting directors. They have been invited as members-at-large to the Academy for more than thirty years, but AMPAS is finally officially acknowledging the importance of their services.

And casting directors' importance will only grow, because as the new-digital media dictates, there continues to be more and more places in which to find actors. This is something you actors know well as you go about preparing your narrative as per the suggestions in this book.

Here's a perfect example of a casting director having an expertise I would never have, and how she saved the day:

We were scouting for a teen actress for our film *Manny & Lo*. We interviewed many young actresses but could not find one we liked. Our casting director said she knew a girl who would be perfect for the lead, a young actress she had been tracking for a few years. And although that young actress had never played any major role in any film, our casting director had done her research, and told us that this young girl was the one for us. It would be her first starring role—she was only eleven years old, and she would be carrying the entire film on her small shoulders. A huge responsibility. But our casting director was confident in this young girl.

After the audition, Marlen and I were impressed with her acting. Although she was young, we thought she was phenomenal, and we urged the director to hire her immediately. Now mind you, this is someone who was eleven years old and not on anybody's radar (except for our casting director's), so even with our collective knowledge and background in film, more than likely we would have never found her.

Was it worth the risk? Did she pan out?

Just a little. She was Scarlett Johansson.

So I quickly learned the hard and lucky way how important a good casting director really is for your film.

Finding a casting director willing to work with you is not as difficult as it seems. Go to IMDbPro and explore some really high-budget studio films. Locate anyone credited as a "casting associate" for those films and approach them, pitching them your now entirely refined narrative to sell them on you and your film. I've been able to find some really talented casting associates this way, many of whom had spent ample time working for top casting agents. This method is a great way to find people with experience, taste, and in some cases even direct contacts to talent—the holy grail for hiring actors to your project.

Actors

I have the highest regard for all actors, but I have found over the years a marked talent difference between SAG-AFTRA members and nonunion actors. Of course, no generalization is going to hold up in every case, and there are legions of nonunion actors with plenty of skill, but in general you'll find that most don't come close to the skills of union actors.

Often new filmmakers assume they cannot afford union actors. Not so. Recently one of my seminar students spoke to me about casting his first feature film. It was very low budget, but to his credit he was well prepared. He had checked the financial numbers, and had concluded there was no way he could afford to pay union actors.

I asked him if he had spoken to the actors' union before he made this decision. He said there had been no reason to, as all the books he read said it was out of the question.

I asked him what he had to lose by trying. We then worked on putting together his narrative, and he went to the union and explained his situation. They then worked together towards the same goals, of hiring SAG-AFTRA actors within a film's low-budget limitations, and negotiated terms that made it work for all those involved.

The end result?

He is now directing a SAG-AFTRA movie on an ultra-low film budget and thrilled about it. The takeaway here? When you have common goals (in this case, hiring good actors), you will be amazed at what you can do.

Where's the best place to look for actors?

When you look for actors to cast, aim high. Really high. Because this is yet another area of the industry that has shifted radically over the past few years. Recent recalibrations in industry production strategies have absolutely turned the film-making process upside down. Studios are making fewer movies every year—half as many, or fewer by some counts. In addition, most films nowadays are either big budgeted or very low budgeted; the midrange-budgeted film is quickly disappearing, and consequently so are the roles for those wonderful, well-known actors who have acted in those midrange-budgeted films. Which means fewer roles for actors, and a bigger pool of actors from which to hire.

This is an opportunity, because actors need to work. Often. Given the climate, it's amazing what casting opportunities are within reach for even the smallest movie—even shorts—if the role makes sense for the actor in question.

Think unconventionally when you go after actors. Try any-thing (that's legal). When I first started out in the business, I would wait backstage at Broadway plays and approach actors as they were leaving. It was a very successful endeavor, but unfortunately, nowadays, they have become inapproachable.

Out of necessity, I have become an expert in the off-Broadway scene. I look to see which actors have gotten great reviews, and then post myself outside the stage door, refusing to budge until they come out. (Side note: It helps if you actually watch the play first.)

When you approach any actor, have your narrative ready. I can tell you from firsthand experience in recent years that off-Broadway performers in particular are almost always very open. And they are often phenomenally talented, and relatively well known in their own right.

If you do not live in New York or Los Angeles, find the near-est large regional theater, check its upcoming schedule, find the actors you want to approach when they come to town, and then go and make your pitch to them. Bring them your script. Actors love a good piece of material; the key is to get it to them when they're at their most receptive. And you can shoot your project around their acting schedule.

In addition, you can find clips of almost any burgeoning actor on YouTube or somewhere else on the Internet. And do your research. You never know what's going to motivate an actor. Find out what they like to do in their time away from the set. Use that information. If you are making a film about horses, look for an actor who loves horses. No stalking, but a genuine interest in your potential cast will help you find people who will be the most passionate about your film.

You can also do an enormous amount of legwork on IMDb-Pro to find actors you're interested in, as well as their manag-ers. Agents are often very busy and overtaxed, but managers by nature are more approachable. Be direct, considerate, and passionate about your project when you call them. You will often be surprised at the results.

Another great resource for finding actors is commercials. As I mentioned before, we found the lead for my first film in a Subaru commercial. The great thing about commercials is that an expert at a high-level ad agency has already done a good deal of the casting research for you. Think about it: Commercials—especially national commercials—are big-budget affairs. They have the resources to have hundreds, if not thousands, of auditions to find the best possible performer for a very specific type. These are often actors who specialize in communicating emotions, story, and nuance, all in a thirty-second spot. So if an ad agency casts a twenty-five-year-old, funny, chubby guy in their commercial, it's likely he's one of the best twenty-five-year-old, funny, chubby actors you'd ever be able to find.

They're in a commercial, so they'll be easy to track down through the ad agency. And because everyone wants to be in the movies—especially commercial actors—they're going to listen to what you have to say, and will probably be willing to audition for you.

When should you cast your actors?

It's always better to be prepared and have as much locked down as early as possible in your process, so it makes sense to cast your actors immediately, right?

Maybe.

In cases where you are looking to land a more prominent actor, your approach should reflect the points I raised before. A major part of your pitch to any famous actor should emphasize minimizing their active time on the project, ensuring there's no inconvenience for them. Every actor has horror stories about low-budget films that have no food, minivans for dressing rooms, and shooting days that last eighteen hours—all with the reward of starting the entire process over again on the next shoot day, before dawn.

You need to demonstrate that your project is not a nightmare waiting to happen. Make it genuinely clear that you'll limit their shooting days, limit their shooting hours, and ensure their comfort on set. And because their time on your movie needs to be short, it's often the best strategy to approach prominent actors only as close to the shooting date as possible. After all, if they commit to your film eight months in advance and David Fincher calls with a role that films at the same time, it's not going to turn out well for you.

Waiting until late in the process can be a harrowing experience, but well worth it if you are able to get a well-known actor to appear in your film. While name actors may be unnerved that they have to make a decision so quickly, they'll at least know that you are legit, that the project is real (with shoot dates and a schedule), and that you can be taken seriously.

And if they end up passing, the less prominent actors whom you have already auditioned will be available on short notice, so you never lose that window of opportunity. Or at that moment you can reconfigure and start your short at a later date. One of the strengths of a low-budget short is that it is very mobile—you can often reschedule it without suffering major losses, just as long as you don't do it a few days before the shoot.

Do not be afraid or intimidated by your prospective actors—if you've assembled a solid crew, you will have a strong team surrounding you, helping you, making sure you and your vision are protected. I remember a film I was producing years ago, and we had a young actress audition for the lead role. She had done a few television roles, but nothing major in film.

She was beautiful, confident, and brilliant. Her audition blew us away, yet the director did not choose her. While the director could see she was amazing, the director felt the young actress was so smart and willful that she might dominate the set and the creative process. I tried to convince the director differently, that we had a strong crew, and that we would protect the director—that this actress could play the role and take our movie to places we'd never even imagined. The director wouldn't listen, and passed on her.

And the actress moved on. Did she end up having a career?

Does the name Angelina Jolie ring a bell?

I guess not being cast in our movie didn't hurt her career too much.

If you have enough confidence in your work, your skill, and the team you put together, you can conquer just about any of your fears.

It is now second nature to record all auditions. And once you have an actor's audition recorded, with today's new-media environment, you can then view it as many times as you need, and in as many mobile venues as possible (e.g., your laptop, your tablet, your phone, or your watch). Thus you can take the digital audition with you wherever you go, allowing you to show it to as many people as you deem necessary to get an informed opinion. And not just people you know, but anyone you see. Your goal here is to get as many opinions as possible. I worked with a director once who would ask taxicab drivers their opinions of audition tapes he had with him. The aim is to get a diversity of opinion, see if there's a consensus, and then make up your mind. But once again, remember: The film begins and ends with you, and you are the final and ultimate arbiter in all creative decisions.

You are not limited by geography in your search. If you

are really interested in someone who is located far from you, you can always audition them via Skype (A blend of Building Blocks One and Two), and go from there. Skype has been one of the most remarkable audition tools ever created. You can audition, go back and forth, and really get a sense of the actor and the performance. I have used Skype in all aspects of filmmaking, and it has become an essential ally to my filmmaking process.

Part Two: Planning

How the heck am I going to plan all of this?

Planning for preproduction is just like the hiring process we covered in part 1 of this chapter.

Here are the first things you have to do.

Sit down and create storyboards and shot lists with your cinematographer.

A storyboard is like a comic strip—you draw images in the sequence as they appear in your script in order to help you visualize your film. Seeing this in front of you as you are in preproduction is invaluable, as it is the first example of what your film will actually look like. And adding weeks to prep for your storyboard and your shot list is cheap compared with the enormous (and usually prohibitive) cost of adding time once you start shooting. Creating storyboards of your film will get you collaborating with your cinematographer. You'll develop a shorthand and comfort level, and it will give you a creative bedrock to fall back upon when you start shooting.

Start scouting locations that you may want to use for your film as you develop your working relationships with your crew.

This might seem obvious but for the wrong reasons. Sure, film-makers have to look at locations as they work up the creative blueprint for their film. But what's equally important and often ignored is that using this time and effort to search for locations also gives you the very first opportunity to work out your relationships with key personnel.

Preproduction is the best time to start shaping the contours of your interactions with your key team members—discovering how to motivate them, what their strengths and weaknesses are, and how much responsibility you can give them—even if you realize that you've made a mistake in hiring them and may eventually need to change horses.

We can talk all we want about creativity, technology, and marketing—but it's in the trenches, during the actual production, where your success will depend entirely on your crew and your relationships with them.

Have your legal agreements completed.

Another overlooked aspect of filmmaking—one that can come around to bite you in the rear down the road—is the necessary legal agreements. It's boring, it's uncreative, it requires attention to detail, and it's the last thing you want to do as you gear up for your movie, but it absolutely has to be done.

You can use fairly standard, boilerplate agreements, but you need to get any commitments made by your cast, crew, and you in writing and signed. In particular, always make sure to include reshoots and ADR (automated dialogue replacement: redoing audio tracks synchronized to the picture) in your contracts. While some actors may not be able to commit to specific dates to do reshoots and/or ADR, it's still smart to employ what's called "reasonable industry standards" language. As always, it's best to consult your inexpensive lawyer about all the legal agreements you'll need for your film.

Rehearse, rehearse, rehearse.

Rehearsal time is relatively inexpensive. On-set time isn't. That's why it's best to do it *before* you're wasting significant money and valuable minutes when you're already in production.

Rehearsals also allow you to get to know your actors. One of the biggest concerns a first-time director has is how to win the respect of his or her cast. The best way to do this is by working directly with them during rehearsals; they will then begin to see your command of the material, which is a great way to earn the approval and respect of a performer.

I was once working with a first-time director who was very reserved and soft spoken. He was terrified that, because of his quiet demeanor, he would not gain the respect of his actors. Granted, he initially came across as shy and unassuming, but when he spoke about his script to me, he became another person. His eyes lit up, his voice rose, and his body language changed into that of a leader. I recorded him once while he spoke about his script, and his passion surprised the heck out of him. I told him to use that person, that "mini-narrative," with his actors during rehearsal, and all would be fine. And it was.

There are different theories of how to run rehearsals. Some filmmakers do not believe in formal rehearsals, believing that the best work comes out in improvisation and spontaneity (particularly in comedies).

I am often asked if you can rehearse too much, draining

your scenes and performances of their energy and potential for invention. The answer always comes back to this: Know yourself. Which process are you most comfortable with? Clint Eastwood sometimes has no rehearsals, whereas at the other end of the spectrum, filmmaker Ingmar Bergman used to rehearse ad nauseam. He wanted the actors to rehearse the material so thoroughly that when it came time to film, they were practically bored with their scenes. Bergman felt it enabled actors, during the actual performance, to stretch even further and transcend the material, finding something fresh and exciting that made a strong addition to the scene. This is not for everyone, but a viable choice nonetheless.

The same applies to the choice of whether or not to shoot the rehearsals as a blueprint for your film—do whatever you think will help your creative process the most. Sometimes it makes actors feel too self-conscious, sometimes it does not. It's your call, depending upon the material, the actors, and your time schedule.

Figure out your budget.

A budget is the backbone of any film production. However, most readers can be surprised at how little money it takes to make a film. Do your research—you can find tons of budgets online, and look into finding more of them from your peers. Find them, take them apart, and adapt one as best you and your line producer can manage.

Not only is your budget your personal guide when making creative and logistical decisions, but it can also be used as one of your greatest sales tools. You should show it to as many people whom you want favors from as necessary. Once they see how economical and fair you are, and that no one is getting more money (or any money!) than anyone else, it can be one of the most persuasive tools in order to ask people to help.

An example of making your budget attractive to your potential investor is to show your financial creativity within your budget. Specifically, when I only had under $75,000 while creating the budget for *Spanking the Monkey,* I was able to approach a local YMCA in the area where we intended to shoot and offer to shoot a promotional video for them in return for having them house our entire crew during the production. They asked to first read our script (mind you, a script about incest), and then they would get back to us. We held our breath for a few days, and then they called back and agreed to the terms. So David O. Russell and I made them their promotional video, and in return we did not have to pay for any housing. And showing that ingenious agreement to prospective investors helped us raise a little more money for our film.

And always map out a workflow postproduction budget, so you'll know for sure what formats your film will end up on. This will be particularly important when you want to release your film, when your distributors give you their list of "deliverables."

End users have many different deliverable requirements, which are the final elements of a film production that the distributor needs in order to exhibit your project, such as the final, fully sound-mixed version of your film on a DVD, separated audio tracks, a press kit, etc. This may seem daunting to the uninitiated, but your line producer or postproduction supervisor can assist you, or if you have to do it yourself, the distributor can be helpful to you as well. But it should be included in your budget.

And make sure to budget in extra days for reshoots. Often

on a low-budget film you cannot get everything you need during your original days of production. But budgeting a few additional days for after you've finished shooting your principal production, and after you've had the time to look at your material, is a major asset that is often overlooked.

Determine which kinds of cameras you'll use.

Probably no on-set tool has changed as radically as the camera over the last generation (Building Block Two). With the advent of digital, cameras have become smaller, lighter, more nimble, and more powerful than ever. The industry is overflowing with new, exciting, and increasingly affordable choices. But remember: There are pros and cons to every camera.

Shooting digital is easy, but its value is sometimes compromised by imparting a digital look that might not be right for your film. Likewise, cheaper cameras and lenses might not have the same key features and extras that pricier models have, and may at times be more awkward to shoot with.

Digital footage is also ultimately easier to manipulate in postproduction. You can zoom in, reframe, and tweak what you've got in a way that you can't (at least not as easily) with film. However, with this new freedom comes responsibility. Knowing you can shoot forever, or correct for some production mistakes in postproduction, creates the potential for enormous problems and enormous costs.

Furthermore, because the digital shooting equipment is so new, all of the workflow issues in postproduction are not uniformly standardized, consistent, or worked out, and it becomes critical that your cinematographer and you work out all of these potential issues ahead of time and don't wait to encounter them while you are in postproduction.

I will not profess to know what the right camera is for your film. But I am here to tell you that we are in the golden age of camera equipment, that we have never had so many choices with which to shoot our films, and that we should fully take advantage of it. (Again, more on digital cameras in chapter 7, which deals with specific issues that have a practical impact on your production while you are actually shooting).

A major caveat. Do *not* choose your cinematographer solely because he has a camera that he will donate to the production. I have seen people make this choice, and it rarely turns out well.

Search the world for your special-effects team.

We recently found a wonderful special-effects company in Eastern Europe. And aside from having some conference calls with them at three a.m. New York time, the work increased the production value of the film tenfold and brought it in *under* budget, at a number that was quite economical. It did take some time getting used to working through our cultural differences, but it was well worth it in the end.

Regarding cultural differences, anytime we wanted them to create an image, we would tell them what it was, but, more important, we would then e-mail them a picture of what that image looks like. We spent too much time in the beginning trying to explain what an American farm silo was to an urban Eastern European; everything moved much quicker when we e-mailed them a picture of the exact farm silo that we wanted for our film.

Technological advances now give you the opportunity to work with talented and budget-saving people from around the world.

Preproduction is an exciting time. You are starting to really make your film. And now you will be prepared to take care of any obstacles that come your way.

Speaking of obstacles, let's look back to my directorial debut. When we left off, I had a pretty major hurdle to overcome, having to find a first AD and AD crew within forty-eight hours or risk shutting down the entire production.

> It was Friday night, and Marlen was calling everyone she knew, looking for the proverbial needle in a haystack—that elusive first AD. We were asking for the impossible—someone to come aboard without any prep time (assistant directors typically get three to six weeks), and to take very little money for the job. And did I mention we needed them to bring on his or her entire staff as well?
>
> As long as I live, I will never forget those two days. We were at the end of January, experiencing one of the coldest NYC winters on record. It was outright freezing, rainy, and bleak. Dark, bone-chilling East Coast weather that just about perfectly matched our emotions at that moment. It seems like all was lost on the film. Losing days of production on a low-budget film is the equivalent of cutting material, as there's never the money to shoot more if you miss something. It was a pivotal moment in my career.
>
> Fortunately, Marlen is relentless and a genius in solving problems. She found us an AD. And an entire AD team.
>
> On Sunday morning, Marlen and I walked into our offices and met Rich Greenberg, our new first AD, and his six-person crew, all waiting to meet, and eager to help us out.

It was a moment that remains one of the highlights of my filmmaking career. The sense of passion and commitment they all had, the sense of wanting to help out, spoke about their character and the respect they had for Rich. And they did not look to take advantage of our situation. Rich knew we needed help, and, with no questions asked, he offered it. He and his team did an amazing job, and I shall always be indebted to him and his team.

You go through your whole life and meet few people like Rich Greenberg. I am happy to say that more than a decade later, he has become a preeminent writer/director, an Emmy Award winner, and is also one of my dearest friends and creative collaborators. This industry is lucky to count him among its members, and anyone would be lucky to work with him.

So amidst all the craziness in the filmmaking business, please remember that (1) all problems are solvable in one way or another, and that (2) there are some remarkably talented and genuine people out there—you just have to seek them out.

Was I lucky? Of course. But we worked hard to get that luck.

Stories like this also make you realize that regardless of how much you plan, or how strong and smart your planning is, at the end of the day you are still dealing with human beings and human emotions (hey, we're not making umbrellas here).

So no matter how much you feel you are prepared, be certain that all you can exactly plan is that things will never go exactly as planned. There's always a hitch. And another. And another. The most important thing to realize here is that things will *always* go wrong.

You have to acknowledge and accept this fact, and then you can learn to think fast on your feet in solving these problems. It may not be 100 percent solvable to your expectations, but it will be resolved in one form or another as you continue moving forward in making your film. And doing strong preproduction as best as you can greatly reduces the odds of things going wrong while you create a successful film and filmmaking experience.

So although the AD problem surfaced in preproduction, we solved it in production. These two stages, preproduction and production, are naturally intertwined, which segues into the next chapter.

You are now ready to shoot your movie. At this point, there is *definitely* no turning back.

PRODUCTION

Making Your Film

Story Number One: The Housekeeper Who Wouldn't Budge

Recently, my son Tyler was directing his first short film. He had been around enough of my productions to know how to prepare, so he had done a really good job in pre-production. He'd assembled a great crew, done his best to anticipate any problems that might come up, made sure he was organized, and readied himself both creatively and logistically. Having locked down his main set location, he approached the first day of his shoot with a strong sense of confidence and excitement.

Tyler woke up early, eager to start the day. He went to his headquarters in Manhattan, and he and his crew began to load the equipment to travel to the apartment he had secured for shooting that day. It didn't take long for the wheels to start coming off. The apartment's long-time housekeeper had planted herself in the entryway, informing my son that she did not know who he was or what he was doing there, and she refused them entry. My son explained that he had approval from her boss—the owner of the apartment—but the housekeeper refused to budge.

Tyler tried calling the apartment owner but couldn't reach her. The equipment was now stacked up in the hallway, and his entire crew was waiting. They could not get in, and the clock had started on his first shoot day. Time and money lost now could never be recouped. And for a low-budget short, that probably meant termination of the project.

What was he to do?

You've got a little more insight about what to do when problems like this arise. But this is a particularly tricky situation: When you select a location, you make specific choices about how to set-dress, light, and shoot that particular site.

Tyler turned to one of his best friends and coproducer of the film, who happened to live with his family in an apartment across town. They quickly decided to move the shoot and adjust the plan. They'd dress the set as best they could while preserving what they could of the lighting plan and shooting approach. They'd lose time moving across town and would have to accommodate the building's lower ceilings, but staying put and arguing with the immovable force of a determined housekeeper was time down a sinkhole.

Fortunately for Tyler, his crew was small, their equipment eminently portable, and they were able to make the move with minimum difficulty. And Tyler was so comfortable with his script, actors, crew, and vision, that he was able to make the transition without too much trouble.

Sure, he lost some assets he would have had in his

original set, but he also gained many new ones by thoroughly exploring the new location. I am not suggesting everyone follow a similar course of action, but if you have command of your material and are comfortable and flexible with your crew, creative adjustments like this can sometimes be a wonderful jolt of energy to your production.

Story Number Two: A Sunday Emergency Call at the Hospital

I once hired a seasoned location manager to work for our crew. He had made sure to secure all the locations for us in preproduction, so we felt we were set.

The middle of the schedule included a week of shooting in a hospital. We arrived early on a Sunday morning to unload our equipment. By now you've realized that I'm beginning each chapter with a good disaster story and you can guess where this is going—we discovered that no one at the hospital knew anything about our film, and under no circumstances would they allow us to set up and shoot. Ugh.

The first thing I did was to call the location manager and ask, "What gives?" It turned out that while he had gotten the hospital administrator's approval, and had sent them the agreement, the hospital had neglected to sign and send the paperwork back to the location manager. Whose fault was it? At that particular moment, determining fault was the last thing on my mind. The bigger issue to solve on that Sunday morning was what to do with my crew of fifty and the street full of equipment trucks waiting to unload and shoot the film's most important scene.

Unlike Tyler's shoot, this was not a small, nimble crew with a single van. But I, too, was now on the clock, burning money and minutes while the crew stood around awaiting instructions.

We politely asked to speak to the weekend administrator, to whom we wished to calmly and thoughtfully explain our situation. As you know, it is my belief that most of the time, if your approach is open, considerate, and respectful, people will want to give you a break and will do their best to help you out if possible.

And that's what happened. Although it was a Sunday, the hospital was kind enough to call the administrator at his home. We spoke to him, he acknowledged the oversight, and he let the hospital know it was okay to allow us to unload and start our shoot.

Production: The Big Kahuna

From these two situations, there are a few facts that every production should take to heart when planning for a shoot. Given the huge number of moving parts on a given day of filming, it's inevitable that, at some point, something is going to go off the rails. And you just have to accept this fact. This is similar to preproduction, but during production the mistakes can possibly be terminal. As you can see in these stories, the problems you encounter on a film, no matter how high or low the budget may be, need exactly the same problem-solving skills.

One of the most remarkable things about the film industry is that we give filmmakers with no business experience the responsibility of running a complex company of many parts with a limited budget, where often many mistakes cannot be fixed; if you make a mistake and then cannot shoot certain scenes, you cannot get those scenes back. If you mess up on two days of your shoot and your shoot is twenty days, you have just irretrievably lost 10 percent of your film. You can try to raise additional funds to do reshoots, but that is a hard road to travel, with results often leaving the filmmaker and his or her film wanting.

And when the films get larger in budget, the stakes get even higher. I was once producing a decently budgeted film in a small town out west. And the evening before one of our leads was to start, we received a call from our distributor back east telling us that we couldn't start shooting until he approved our lead's hairstyle. We had pictures to show the distributor, but this was before the time of the Internet, and the last overnight delivery service for the night had already left from our small town. If we did not get his approval before the next morning, we could not shoot that day, and would lose tens of thousands of dollars and also lose some important scenes due to the limitations in the actor's time availability.

After researching for a while, it came down to two choices. We found out there was an airplane freight service a few hours away in a major city that was leaving in a few hours. If we could make that flight, then the package would arrive the next morning, and the distributor could see the hairstyle first thing in the morning, and if it was okay we could start shooting without missing a beat.

And if we missed the flight, I had the car filled with four company employees, who would switch off driving through the night to get back east as soon as possible to have the distributor view the pictures.

The good news is that we made the airplane freight service,

the distributor signed off on the hairstyle pictures, and we were able to continue shooting that morning.

Of course you have to learn to think on your feet, but more important, once you realize how ridiculously lopsided the business parameters are in relationship to the product you are making as a filmmaker, then you'll be able to give yourself some slack—it is not you, but the system that is crazy. And sure, these stories ended up well, but there are many more that did not. And the biggest mistake I have found is that once something disastrous happens, the inexperienced filmmaker becomes defeated, the obstacle seemingly too personal and great, and the ultimate product, if even completed, suffers greatly.

So be aware that the odds are uniquely stacked against you during production. Ride out the storm and know that you're not alone; I cannot begin to tell you how many times I have seen mistakes made and then turned around to become some of the best parts of the final film.

Major Considerations When Making the Best Movie You Can

There are a multitude of components in a film production shoot, and I will highlight the most significant ones for you to get the best possible film that you can.

Digital

Using a digital camera is easily the most important technical element in your film. I touched on digital cameras in the prior chapter on preproduction, and will go further in depth here because of their major prominence in the actual film shooting.

Digital cameras have revolutionized filmmaking because they are so inexpensive to rent or buy, and so easy to use, making them accessible to just about everyone. So there is a very strong chance you'll be shooting your first film with a digital camera. But beware, as the ease of digital can sometimes yield unexpected liabilities during production.

Digital cameras essentially shoot by storing your footage electronically, like a computer. While filming, it allows you to shoot many sequences, in continuous takes, which can go on for hours. With traditional film, you are limited in what you can shoot to several minutes before you must reload the "film magazine" on the camera. Digital cameras are also significantly lighter and more mobile than film cameras, giving you enormous flexibility in how you approach the scene you want to shoot. And you have additional enormous savings by not having to continually buy expensive film stock.

Thinking you have no limitations when shooting with a digital camera can make you less precise in your craft, subconsciously slackening the creative muscle. I have seen this happen over and over again. And this does not simply apply to directors. When everyone, from actors to other key personnel, knows that you can shoot and reshoot forever, or manipulate the footage in postproduction, some may adopt the attitude that they don't need to work to make things perfect on the set. Sometimes the feeling is that we don't have to get it perfect right away, because we can always do it again, or "fix it" in post.

No one wins with that way of thinking, and that type of thinking explodes your postproduction budget. Your job as a filmmaker is to manage limits within the freedom that digital gives you. Although your instinct may be to allow the cinematographer or actor a wide berth here, that freedom can quickly turn into excess, and you'll ultimately find yourself asking, "What am I going to do with all this footage?" It is unwieldy, imprecise, and a waste. Sometimes too many choices result in no choices.

Playback

There is no excuse for not having a playback monitor on your set, which is what it says it is, a monitor on your set that plays back the scene you just shot. It is inexpensive and allows you to quickly see what you have just shot. But here, too, you must be acutely aware of the pros and cons of this equipment.

The benefits are obvious. You can review your footage immediately, right on set. This can help you make decisions, determine whether you have gotten the shot you want, and double-check that there are no mistakes, such as an errant camera, boom mic, or lights accidentally creeping into your shot. When used properly, playback is invaluable as a creative facilitator, and can save you many headaches down the road.

On the flip side, your work is now open to perusal and opinions from all those around you on the set. And at times, too many cooks do spoil the broth. Consider the new decisions you will have to make: Will you allow an actor to review playback—particularly directly after his or her take? At times you may not even have the ability to control what happens. The actor may simply look, regardless of what you think. In general, I believe that this decision of who has access to the playback should be dependent upon the situation, meaning if the actor's involvement and consequent point of view is constructive to the process, fine. But if he or she gets to be obstructive, or takes up an inordinate amount of time, then it is best to try to keep the playback just for the director's use.

I also find many first-time filmmakers end up glued solely to the monitor while the actor is giving his or her performance.

They often argue that, since the monitor more accurately reflects the final product, all attention should be focused there and not on the actor. I understand this way of thinking, but you have to remember that you are dealing with an actor, a live human being who is in search of feedback and support. The monitor comes between the actor/director relationship physically and metaphorically. They'll know when you're watching their face and eyes and when you're watching the monitor. And with that knowledge, one can breed insecurity or misplaced focus.

In a similar vein, I've seen situations where directors become so dependent on playback that they begin neglecting the actors right in front of them by obsessively checking each take.

Furthermore, you should always be mindful of the amount of time that can be lost discussing and viewing the takes on set. Remember, as crude as it sounds, on a movie set, time is money.

It becomes a very delicate balancing act, one you will figure out early on in the process of your production.

Dailies

Dailies were originally considered the first prints made by the laboratory from the footage shot the day before. With digital footage, things have changed, but the idea is still the same. To go to a large screening room to watch what you have shot, particularly when you have already seen it on a playback monitor, may seem excessive and costly. However, I have found the process of reviewing dailies on a larger screen at least a few times during your shooting schedule to be well worth the time, money, and effort. Screening dailies accomplishes three main purposes at the same time:

1. There is *nothing* like seeing your film on a large screen
    to get a real sense of what's going on visually. This goes
    back to the theory of why people love movies: Despite
    the proliferation of people watching films on monitors,
    watches, phones, etc., I truly believe that the real magic
    of movies is revealed in this format; that it all starts
    with us watching huge images collectively in a dark
    room. And by watching your dailies— huge images in
    a dark room—you will see things in your footage you
    couldn't have seen before. On the creative end, your
    actors' performances will read differently, you'll be
    able to see the frame in greater detail, and you'll be able
    to notice nuances in what you've captured that are too
    subtle for a small screen. On the technical side, you'll
    be able to catch things like focus issues and continu-
    ity errors, and what might be hidden in the background
    will show up in ways that give you much more insight.

2. Remember the Marlen Hecht school of filmmaking,
    acknowledging the three films you make when you
    make your one film: the script, the shoot, and the edit?
    Watching dailies or screening quick rough edits of
    scenes can reveal new things in your footage; it can
    also sometimes trigger new ideas and creative inspira-
    tions that lead to unexpected changes in the script—
    either to fix things that seem problematic, or to
    expand on elements that are working better than you'd
    originally anticipated. And being that you are doing
    this during production, you can then incorporate any
    useful information, if necessary, to alter the course of
    your production.

    I remember watching dailies on *Flirting with
    Disaster*. The story was moving along very well, and

we were happy with the shoot. However, as we started coming closer and closer to the conclusion of production, the dailies made it clear that we were looking at a different movie than the script initially called for. We realized then that the original ending wouldn't work, as it was too conventional for the type of film we were watching on the screen. Luckily, we had a wonderful ensemble of actors who got along really well with each other in a screwball, crazy, beautiful way.

Noting this—how *every* character in the film had become part of a crazy dysfunctional family—I asked why we couldn't simply make the ending something short and sweet. I suggested having a visual of everyone getting together for a final family snapshot, freeze framing on the picture, then you physically zoom out to realize that it is an actual photo, and then using that to end the movie. So, despite our original plans, the footage I saw on the dailies triggered the creative inspiration to allow me to make the suggestion I did.

And guess what the ending of the film was?

Yes, the still photograph.

3. There are also many smaller benefits to screening dailies. Having the crew get together on occasion to see dailies is a great way to sustain the camaraderie and feelings on set. It's a bonding experience. The same way you want to see your own work so too, will your crew. They'll want to know if their camera work was seamless, if the makeup they designed holds up on film, or how the colors in their set-dressing look in the frame. Most people you hire on your crew are a little like mini-filmmakers in their own discipline. They've

worked very hard, and rather than wait months and months to see the fruits of their labor, they can see pieces of it soon after they helped create it. And don't waste time fearing they may not like it.

But beware, as Francis Ford Coppola said, "A finished film never looks as good as the dailies, or as bad as the first cut."

Shooting Your Scenes

A director takes care of many tasks while he or she is working on the set. The director must be a leader, auteur, collaborator, psychologist, and all-around cheerleader. Here are additional central issues to think about as you prepare for your actual shoot.

Actors

How many takes do you anticipate for each scene? The decision about the number of takes you need becomes a question primarily of time management; shooting more takes extends the day and schedule, ultimately costing the production money. The number of takes also has to be balanced against the creative process; will having many takes slow down the creative atmosphere? Or will having more takes give the film more opportunities for great performances? David Fincher shoots tens (and sometimes hundreds) of takes; Clint Eastwood shoots two or three. When shooting, you will find your own style and pace.

You'll find out quickly what your actors can give you, as well as their performance peculiarities. Some actors need constant reinforcement while others only get worse the more you advise them. Likewise, some actors are always best on the first take, and others may need extensive repetition to get where they need to go for their best work.

If you have followed my principles, by the time you're shooting, you'll have spent a good deal of time with your actors in rehearsals, so you'll know how to get the best performances out of everyone.

Filming

Actors can be very supportive. I remember once, during my directorial debut, an actress came up to me after a take and whispered to me, "Dean, by working with you in all those rehearsals, I know you are a very strong director, and I have complete faith in you. But here's a point of advice: When you say 'action' to begin a scene, say it with strong conviction! These are the first words actors hear before we start our performance, and the more emphatic you are, the more confident we become in your skills." Great advice, and I have always remembered it. Again, sometimes it's the little things that make the biggest difference.

Start rolling film (or start recording, if you're using digital) before you say "action," and continue rolling or recording for a little while after you have said "cut." I say this for three specific reasons: (1) shooting digital, it won't cost that much more to use additional storage space; (2) sometimes the best moments come when no one is paying attention—I have gotten some amazing shots this way; and (3) having that extra beginning and tail-end footage really comes in handy in editing, allowing you to control the pace and timing of your film.

How to Maximize Production Value

Production value is one of those phrases used so often it starts to lose meaning, as it applies to almost anything that improves your movie. It goes without saying that everyone wants great production value on a limited budget, but few people really know how to do it; they end up espousing generic, banal truisms (e.g., shoot smart or shoot fast) that are completely useless.

Here are some specific examples illustrating how to maximize production value on a limited budget.

Locations

If you can source very accurate locations, you can save money on dressing the scene and enhance the look of your production. And if you are really lucky, you can shoot many of your scenes in different rooms of the same location, saving a remarkable amount of time and money. If you're shooting outside a house for a scene, use the inside for any location that could work, even if it's supposed to be a distant physical space in your film's story. You can dress any room to resemble almost any location—a doctor's office, a bedroom, a coffee shop.

On *Spanking the Monkey,* for example, we found one big house in Pawling, New York, and were able to shoot just about all of our interior scenes there. Without that house, there was no way we would have been able to complete the film on our $75,000 budget. However, as evidenced by the opening two stories of this chapter, securing locations can be a very perilous venture in a film. No matter how you try, sometimes things can get out of control.

In a film I recently produced, we had everything set to shoot in a house we wanted in upstate New York. Similar to *Spank-*

ing the Monkey, we had planned to shoot many of our scenes in front of this house. It was one of our linchpin locations.

Unlike the earlier stories, we had all the signed agreements and were in constant touch with the owners, and after a week of shooting in the house, everything went according to plan.

This, you know by now, is the first sign of trouble.

We started shooting outside on their lawn early Saturday morning. It was our last day and, as I mentioned, production had been remarkably trouble free so far. Film sets often use pretty heavy equipment—big stands to hold up big lights, for example—and our cinematographer had instructed the crew to take extra care not to do any damage to the exterior of the house or its front lawn.

All of a sudden, we heard police sirens approaching our set. Two policemen jumped out of the car and demanded we stop shooting.

Flummoxed, I asked, "Why?"

Although all of our papers were in order, the cinematographer, while shooting on the lawn, had inadvertently placed some equipment a few inches over the boundary of our approved property and onto that of the next-door neighbor, and they had accused us of trespassing. Because we had broken the law, our original location agreement was nullified.

I thought either he was joking, or I was in the movie *Deliverance*. Turns out it was neither. This was an extreme case, but I'd seen this kind of thing before. People get very territorial when it comes to property, and sometimes become jealous of neighbors who are getting location fees for use of their property. Whatever the case, the next-door neighbor filed a claim, and because it was Saturday, there was no one to whom we could register our appeal.

My first approach was to speak to the neighbor. He had filed the claim the prior day, and I found he was not at home. (Later on we found out that he was just fired from his job and was angry at the world, and we were simply in the wrong place at the wrong time.) So much for direct, honest discussions.

I knew we couldn't afford to stop shooting. The schedule was too tight, and our resources were already spread too thin. It was our last day shooting at the house, and we just needed a few more hours. We were due to begin at another location on Monday, and we had no rights, time, or money to expand the shoot.

Luckily, we had a backup plan—an emergency rip cord we would pull only as a last resort. This, clearly, was such a situation.

On our first arrival to this small town, we went directly to the nearby fire department and police department, introduced ourselves to them, and told them where and when we would be shooting, and to let us know if our film caused problems of any kind. We explained honestly that we knew film productions could sometimes be inconsiderate and disruptive, and causing problems was the last thing we wanted to do.

Being a low-budget film with limited resources, one of our strongest assets was courtesy and politeness. But that genuine token of good faith on our part really came in handy. We explained our production predicament to the policemen we were speaking with, and asked them to call our liaisons at the fire and police departments for a reference check on our good intentions. They made a few calls, said they'd be back, and drove away. We finished our shoot in the next few hours, never heard from them again, and all was good. Rip cord pulled, bullet dodged.

Shot Lists, Storyboards, and Coverage

I discussed shot lists and storyboards in the preproduction chapter; this is where those items pay off. Use your shot lists and storyboards to schedule how you will cover your scenes, which means setting up enough shots for each scene so that it will flow well during editing. This will then become one of the director's greatest assets while shooting. You will almost always feel the instinct to shoot more: more takes, new setups, and different angles. The more you get, the more choices you will have in postproduction. Having more footage allows for more possibilities in the *right hands of a strong director and editor,* and can make a film's potential explode.

And if you have the extra time and everyone is still available, just shoot anything else that you think is interesting—you never know what you can end up using.

But also remember that more shots take more time and more money, in production and eventually in postproduction. Shooting your first scene over and over will likely jam you for time, and you may find you have to cut material. Your initial plan may have been to shoot a new scene in seven shots, but now you might find you need to find a way to do it in five. Or three. Or even one.

"A Great Movie Moment"

In a low-budget film, it is sometimes prudent to spend a lot of time, money (relatively speaking), and energy to shoot one big scene. Big, complex shots eat up time on a set, but that extra time is occasionally worth budgeting for. There may be key moments in your film that need to transcend budget and shooting limitations—ones that can send your work soaring to another level.

Remember, film is larger than life. You have to find a way to transport the audience, no matter how "small" your film may seem to be. It is not the size that counts. (I know you've heard that saying before, but it is *really* true here!) Every film, no matter how big or small, must have some bona fide "movie moments"—sequences that shatter your audience's expectation and flood them with hope or fear, happiness or dread. Find that moment in your film, and then build what I call your "trailer shot" (a shot so cinematic and interesting you know it has to be in the trailer) around it.

Trailer shots not only serve to elevate your film, but can also serve as a major part of any promotional visuals for your film.

And if you're lucky, you may be able to solve a few problems at the same time. Things could play out like this:

As we were shooting *Spanking the Monkey,* we had already located our trailer shot in the script. In the penultimate scene of the film, it is implied that the protagonist, Raymond (Jeremy Davies), will try to kill himself. It was a crucial scene, and, despite our entire budget of $75,000, we still rented a huge crane, allowing us to capture Davies standing atop a huge quarry, looking down towards his death. It was a huge scene, and, relatively speaking, cost a ridiculous amount. But we knew it had the potential to sell the movie . . . and it did. It proved to be money very well spent.

And as we got closer to filming the scene, I kept pondering how we could make our money shot even more impactful without increasing the cost of the shoot. As I stood there that night, watching the setup for the jump, it came to me. I recalled a time—believe it or not—when I once fell over a cliff. As I careened down the mountain towards my possible death (which is a whole other story), I saw my whole life flash before my eyes, as weird as that sounds. It was one of the strangest things that had ever happened to me.

So I suggested to David O. Russell, the director, that we edit together a quick succession of cuts from the character's life— all material we'd already shot—and intercut that with his jump, stylistically simulating our hero experiencing his life flash before his eyes when he leaps. It would enhance our trailer shot and wouldn't cost the film another dime. We did it, and it ended up being very effective.

Audio

Sound is almost always ignored or given short shrift in lower-budget productions. Even though unsophisticated viewers might not notice you've scrimped on your sound package by using a cheap boom instead of a lavalier mic, their ears will *absolutely* spot the use of low-quality audio equipment or other shortcuts. And not in a good way.

There are visual glitches in every movie, small breaks in continuity or cuts that don't quite match. The human eye is actually very forgiving of these small mistakes. The human ear, however, is *not*. Film audio has to be seamless, or everyone will notice something is wrong. It is extraordinary that some filmmakers don't pay attention to this critical fact. It could be that most filmmakers are trained to think of film as a visual medium, but the fact remains that simple oversights in audio can turn into huge mistakes. Bad sound (e.g., echoey, tinny, windy, no "room" tone, too low, hollow soundings, etc.) is one of the biggest problems I have seen in low-budget film-making. And once recorded incorrectly, sound cannot really be fixed.

Sure, it's a little time consuming and an economic pain to mic everyone, use a boom, and play every scene back to make sure it sounds perfect. But if you don't, there *will* be audio mistakes, and some may be so obvious that they could really make your film suffer; others may require you to clean up background sound, a process that can be very costly. It would be a real tragedy if someone disliked your film just because of a subtle audio glitch that he or she isn't even experienced enough to precisely identify—especially because such a problem is so easily preventable on set.

Editing

As often as it is practicable, have your editor work alongside you during the actual shooting period of your film. Seeing an edited scene, even a rough cut, can really make a difference; it can help you see how your actors are coming across and help you develop your coverage strategy—that is, how you will shoot your next scenes, and what material you may need to go back and reshoot. If possible, ask your editor to add a temporary music track to the scene. By starting the editing process early, you can quickly progress the film's schedule and find out if your vision is aligned with the editor's. If the two of you do not see eye to eye on the rough cut, you can always work with him or her to try to overcome those differences, thus saving time by being in agreement earlier in the process.

Special Effects

I have discussed special effects with regards to preproduction, and here is where the special-effects work you have done in preproduction pays off. If you've created a dialogue with your special-effects team, they will be very well prepared to set up your special effects during your production. You will be amazed at how inexpensive they can be and how much value they will add to your film when used appropriately.

In production, these are the major elements to pay attention to. Obviously there will be many other components that come into play, but gaining skill in these major components will help you enormously.

And now for something completely different . . . (but not really).

Promotion and Marketing During the Shoot

Now, you may ask, why am I all of a sudden talking about promotion and marketing in the middle of a chapter dealing with production? Well that is *exactly* the point. This is the *ideal* time to set up the beginnings of your promotion and marketing campaign, when you are shooting, when everyone is around, when you can get the most exciting materials to use when your film (short or feature) is complete and ready for the world. On the contrary, it seems crazy to me that filmmakers do not realize this. A little planning ahead, for a lot of return. But no one does this.

However, do not distribute any of these following materials until your film is complete, or has a distributor.

On-Set Digital Still Photography

Still photos of you and your team in action give an inexpensive behind-the-scenes look at preproduction, production, and postproduction, and can become a major asset for your marketing and promotion campaign down the road. These digital photos can be used in your trailer, poster, press kit, website, texts, tweets, sent out to third-party users—their uses are virtually endless.

Video News Release

Inexpensive, well-made digital recorders are so prevalent these days that it's now a simple matter to have someone document your film's production in front and behind-the-scenes. There's no telling what can come out of this process: inspiration for your project, another idea for a film, or even great footage for a mini "making of" piece. At minimum, you will have a video document of the creation of your film, many sections of which will definitely come in handy when promoting it and your career.

Unit Publicist

This sounds a lot more official and expensive—but it isn't. Bring in a friend, or see if you can find a student at a nearby journalism school, and have that person come to your set to create publicity materials (bios of the principals, a story synopsis of the film, photos, video clips, etc.) to be used separately and then all together to create a press kit (to be discussed more in chapter 9).

Website

I have mixed feelings about creating a website. I know that everyone does it; I am just not sure of its value. A badly made website can hurt your film, so if you do create a website, you should start it in preproduction, but you will be getting a great deal of your material during production and postproduction. And make sure it is really done well because your website is often the first thing the outside world sees about your film (and possibly the last). And if you create it, make sure to set it up to interact with social media as you prepare your film for the marketplace.

Things to Avoid in Promotion and Marketing

I have never understood why some filmmakers strive for as much press as possible during the preproduction and production phases of their film. I can see the value of an early coordinated campaign with a major motion picture starring big-name actors, as such films depend on the aura of excitement and anticipation months in advance.

But guess what? That's not your film. You are a first-time filmmaker. When you create a website announcing your short, or try to get press in your local newspaper, most of the time you do nothing to advance your film or your career. If anything, this could actually backfire. Face it: Today, everyone has a website. Your plumber and your babysitter do. Everyone. The industry knows this, so it's no badge of honor. And if you announce your film too early on, and it takes months and months (if not longer) to complete, it's a signal to the industry that says, "This film is a Mickey Mouse operation," or that the production is having problems, or simply that you're an inexperienced filmmaker who knows how to get press better than you can make a film.

I once had first-time filmmaker legal clients who were thrilled to get a notice on Page Six of the *New York Post* announcing the start of their film. Although they were just starting production, they sent that notice to all prospective distributors. I thought that was a bad idea and told them so.

Later, when their film took longer than expected to complete (often the case with first-time filmmakers), people began asking: What's taking so long? Are there problems? These questions adversely affected the filmmakers, creating pressure where there otherwise would have been none. And when the film was ready to be shown to distributors, it was looked at with skepticism. Your goal is to create the optimum environment for a distributor to see your film, and these filmmakers had failed to do so. (We'll look at this in more depth in chapters 9 and 10, which cover marketing after production.)

Whenever promotional efforts become an issue for a film, it is almost always a problem of the filmmaker's own creation. Here you must learn that you are not the only force in control of your narrative. Once the perception of production problems becomes part of your film's story, it's something that's almost impossible to erase. You'll find yourself presenting your project not with optimism, but with the burden of having to overcome the biases among your viewers that something's wrong with your film.

In addition, almost all first-time filmmakers rush to IMDb-Pro to announce their films to the industry the moment they begin preproduction. Why? To what end? So the entire industry can judge them for how long it takes to get out to the marketplace? By publicly announcing your film in this way, you run the risk of its narrative spinning totally out of your control, left forever on IMDbPro for the industry to see as a record of your film that was never finished.

I am not saying you will always be able to manage or control every aspect of the press attention that may come to your film, but you have to try to minimize any pitfalls that may arise. Try not to draw too much spotlight early on, so you can make sure that promotional outlets will see your final product in the best possible light, and hope they respond to it accordingly.

The Martini Shot*

(*Industry speak for the last shot of the day, and in this case, your film)

So congratulations: You have now finished shooting your film. You've reached a place many never see. You may still need to do some reshoots, which I will discuss in chapter 8, but basically you are finished. Finishing is very liberating. Take a deep breath, because now, for the most part, you have the major elements of your film "in the can."

Up until now a good percentage of the elements of your film were out of your control. Strong preproduction helped you attempt to control many of those elements, and you set it up as ably as you could and then hoped for the best.

But now it's different. For the first time in this process since the development of the script, you are going into postproduction, when you are now fully back in charge.

Very exciting, and very terrifying.

Even if you think the shoot went terribly, or if everything else seemed to go wrong, don't stop now. Don't be one of those films whose status says "in postproduction" for years and years, essentially becoming a dead-on-arrival statistic on IMDbPro.

So now is the time to let go of what you initially wrote and see what you now have to work with.

And don't worry if you feel you have done really badly when shooting your film. I have seen my filmmaking partner, Marlen Hecht, save many a film in postproduction, and so can you. Despite having made some mistakes along the way—not always getting the coverage you wanted, or the perfect performance from your actors—you're now about to start postproduction, to reshape your film a final time. And this will be by far the most important phase of your production, because sitting in a room with your raw footage, watching it over and over again, will spark more new ideas and possibilities, allowing you to create something more personal and beautiful than you've been able to in the process thus far.

And if you need any more reason not to turn back consider this:

One of the most instructive lessons I ever learned was found inside John Pierson's file cabinet. John is a filmmaker, was a film rep extraordinaire, now teaches film at the University of Texas, and is the author of the bestselling memoir *Spike, Mike, Slackers & Dykes: A Guided Tour Across a Decade of American Independent Cinema.* Years ago, I asked him how he could feel comfortable pushing people into an industry when chances of failure were so high.

He took me to his file cabinet, opened it, and asked me to peruse its contents. I found myself looking through hundreds of applications John had acquired in which he essentially asked wannabe filmmakers whether they regretted spending a good deal of their money and time on their projects. And a great majority of them, whether they were successful or not, said it was one of the best experiences of their entire lives, and almost as many said that they would do it again in a heartbeat. And that's when it hit me, that old adage: "When you follow what you love to do, it will lead you to where you really want to go." It was true. It's a simple lesson, but one of the most important ones I can give you.

So don't stop now: Edit and make your movie.

POSTPRODUCTION

When Your Film Becomes Your Film

In postproduction you finally have control of your film again. The uncertainties of production have ended, and your tools are simpler—it's just you and your footage now. By and large, the process is much easier to wrangle. The key words in that idea are, of course, "by and large."

As an example of "by and large," W. C. Fields once famously declared that filmmakers should "never work with animals or children." While that's good advice, it's a little limited. He might also have wanted to add music rights in documentaries to that list.

> It was a morning just after Labor Day when the Samuel Goldwyn Company, which was working with us on *Wigstock* (a wonderful feature-length documentary on the annual New York drag festival of the same name), called to say the film had been accepted into the Sundance Film Festival. Great news, right? Not so fast.
>
> Let me back up a bit. The Samuel Goldwyn Company had initially gotten involved in *Wigstock* earlier

that summer on the condition that Marlen and I agreed to spearhead the film's production. The director had shot parts of the Wigstock Festival the previous summer, and Goldwyn had asked us to further develop, produce, and edit the film, as well as to shoot this summer's festival. We didn't have much time for preproduction (the event was just a few weeks away), but we really liked the material, so we thought, why not?

Although Wigstock had a tiny budget, the film was a bear of a project—shot over two summers, using a variety of different formats (film, video, some 8-millimeter) and featuring huge performance pieces, crowds, famous original and lip-synced songs, and intricate dance and musical numbers. On top of all that (and our abbreviated preproduction schedule), we were told we'd have less than 120 days to complete the entire film! It was an insane deadline.

As difficult as it all seemed then, a few months later, deep into our editing and with Sundance on the horizon, things took a drastic turn for the worse.

Much to our shock, we discovered that the rights to use many of the lip-synced or recorded songs we had already edited into the film were not cleared—that is, we did not have the rights to use those songs!

Only weeks away from Sundance, we found ourselves in the unenviable position of having to separate which songs we could and couldn't use. Negotiating new licenses would prove extremely difficult, as we would need to secure permission from performers like Barbra Streisand, Faye Dunaway, the Beastie Boys, and other big-name artists, all in the span of a few weeks.

It immediately became clear that because of elements out of our personal control, some of the sequences we had spent months editing together would be worthless without the songs we'd cut them to. This was not a matter of replacing background music. And in addition, there were also live performance pieces whose music we now had to get the rights to. Marlen and I took to the phones, calling all the right people to get the clearances we needed.

There's a funny thing about deadlines: Most of the time when you explain your situation, people respond to your urgency. Clearing music is one of the most peculiar processes in filmmaking. Often you'll find the most eccentric people controlling certain songs and estates, and there is no rhyme or reason as to whether they will decide to give you the rights or not. We called friends of friends who knew certain performers, tracked down an artist on a distant island, spoke with record labels, and did every other legal thing we could think of to get the rights we needed—all on our extremely limited budget.

To our luck, we managed in every case to either clear the rights or replace the song, for almost every scene of the film. Almost.

It turned out we wouldn't be able to clear one key song, probably the most important song in the film. Naturally it was a song so deeply woven into a pivotal sequence of the film that it was impossible to swap it out. And Sundance was days away.

We asked everybody we knew in the music and audio industry for advice, and here was our ultimate solution: We started working with Peter Fish, a wonderful composer, and went step-by-step through our footage, as well as musical phrase by musical phrase, and even note by note. We arduously replaced the entire song with similarly pitched music, so as to exactly match the picture.

*It was meticulous work, matching every musical tone
and crescendo, while remaining legally distinct from
the existing song. While maddeningly time consuming,
it worked beautifully in the end, and to this day no one
can tell the difference.*

My point?

*We clearly thought we had all the music rights in
preproduction, but it turned out that we did not. Consequently, a major failure in preproduction can be fixed in
postproduction, even under the most arduous of circumstances—an example of why postproduction, under
your control, is the most important aspect of your film.*

Never Underestimate the Importance of Postproduction

Postproduction is truly a make-or-break time for your film. Everything is at stake. Just as you shouldn't be too rigid with your
script while filming, you can't be too rigid with the footage you
shot, either. Your script is your guide when you're editing, but
you have to look at what you shot almost as if it's a second film.

Editors for your film can be found through the suggestions I made in chapter 6. Also, editing is a learned skill, but
the good news is that technology has made editing extremely
user-friendly. So if you have the time and read the right books
and manuals, and do the appropriate research on editing, there
is nothing to stop you from trying your hand at editing, as long
as you have outside collaborators offering objective criticism
of your work.

If there's one lesson to be learned about editing a film, it's
the unbelievable way it can pay off to keep working, experi-

menting, and cutting; there will always be another piece of music to try, or another way to play with a scene. This, as I've mentioned, is why you must leave a healthy portion of your budget for postproduction.

Technology (Building Block Two)

As remarkable as on-set technological advancements have been, they are equally matched by recent innovations in postproduction. This is both a blessing and a curse. Digital editing software makes it incredibly easy to cut, replace, shift around, and do amazing things with the picture and sound on a film, which can be great . . . to a point.

More specifically, digital nonlinear editing has the ability to access, move, and cut frames of your movie through the click of a mouse, without changing or destroying anything. Before digital nonlinear editing, the technology was very rudimentary, and it took a great deal of effort, cost, and time to make changes to the footage you shot and the audio you recorded. The economic realities of the old analogue process forced filmmakers to really think through postproduction choices far in advance. Nowadays you don't need such foresight. What might formerly have cost a lot of money and man-hours editing a scene now costs relatively little, and happens in minutes.

On one hand, this freedom can be liberating: Renting or owning digital picture-editing equipment is relatively inexpensive, and opens up many vistas for your film's growth. But how does one know when to stop? It's a similar issue to the discussion in chapter 7 on shooting in digital: When is enough . . . enough? Practiced self-discipline, as well as listening to the advice of respected collaborators, is always a good place to start when navigating this potentially thorny issue.

The same applies to audio. Technology has become so sophisticated, a filmmaker could tinker, tweak, and finesse the sound of her or his film forever. The upside here is that even an independent film can boast a highly polished soundtrack; often filmmakers do not find audio editing as pleasurable as visual editing, but if there's one area to really indulge in using new technology, it's in perfecting the sound of your film. But here, too, please beware. New filmmaking technology is wonderful, but you must always set reasonable time limits for postproduction audio as well, or you'll burn through your allocated budget.

You now have a roughly edited cut of your film, using the new technologies to your maximum benefit. Where do you go from here?

Evaluating Your Film and Finding a Consensus (The "Rough Cut")

Finding an objective, clear-eyed way to evaluate your film is probably the most overlooked, underestimated, and crucial part of the postproduction process. It's also one of the most difficult to achieve. How is it possible to be objective about a story you've lived with in your mind for months, or even years, for which you've exhausted yourself filming, and are now watching (literally) hundreds of times over as you edit?

Remember the *second* half of Francis Ford Coppola's axiom: "A finished film never looks as good as the dailies, or as bad as the first cut." So don't worry; take a deep breath, and unveil the first cut to the world—or rather, a selective world of your choosing. This early version is going to be flawed. Count on it. But you're about to make it better. Much better.

Screening Your Film

As I mentioned in chapter 7 on production, it is very important to screen your film and experience it in a larger-than-life
format. Even more so once your film has completed shooting.
I am all for saving money, but I am also for spending it smartly.
And if it is too costly for you to screen often on a big screen, you
can also screen on large video screens—anything that is larger
than the screen you have been watching when you have been
editing. Remember our discussion on writing and creativity?
It's the same principle: Moving where you work to a different
venue is a great way to exercise your creative muscles, and it
will absolutely allow you to see your film in a different light.

In addition, invite people to watch your film and ask them
for their opinions. Go online and take a look at some sample
marketing surveys. Review and analyze them, and consider
creating your own survey so that viewers can give you direct
and helpful feedback. But simply having a survey is not enough;
you have to understand how to interpret the responses you get.
Have discussions with the viewers, first individually and then
as a group, to get a better sense of what people thought worked,
and what might have confused, upset, or bored them.

Park your ego at the screening-room door. The most valuable
information you're going to get from a screening is the identifi-
cation of what *isn't* working. It might be uncomfortable to hear,
but you can't fix your film if you don't know what's broken.

It's also important to make sure you screen your film not
only to friends, but also to friends of friends. Pay particular attention to the responses of those less close to you; their
thoughts are often much more telling. Your friends likely know
you very well, and they may have unconscious biases. Their
natural proclivity will be to support you, and thus they may not

be as critical of your film as they should be. At the end of the day, your most important goal is to find a consensus among all the comments.

Obviously this isn't an arithmetic formula, and you shouldn't make reflexive changes without mulling them over, but always pay attention when a single issue is flagged by several individuals. Remember, you always have to balance those twins of filmmaking: your personal aesthetic and the market appeal of your film. The responses from your screening will be your first look at how your movie is going to play to audiences.

Here's where things can get a little tricky. A layperson may comment that he or she doesn't like the protagonist in a particular scene, but as is often the case, the issue may not be in that exact scene, but in certain scenes leading up to that scene. For example, if someone is not believing the motivation of a character in a particular scene in your movie, often there is a good chance that the problem started in earlier scenes, when you were originally creating your character and his or her motivations.

The principles for review and response are very similar to the principles found in chapters 2 ("Development") and 3 ("The Script"). Done the right way, a system of outside feedback for evaluating your creative work is always useful, no matter what stage of the creative process you're in.

So now you've done some creative calisthenics and built up your critical "muscles" from holding screenings. This is the first time since you worked on your script that you'll be able to majorly restructure and change your product. You're going to trim, reshuffle, reshape—change the tone of performances, build better editorial rhythms—and if necessary, to start planning to go back and reshoot certain scenes, or shoot additional scenes.

Remember to be wary of the costs involved in staging re-shoots, but know that sometimes it's the only way to fix problems that are holding your work back.

Sam Goldwyn Jr. once said the two most important parts of a film are its beginning (where you "set the table," getting people excited about the plot) and its ending. The final emotions audiences are left with as they exit the theater are influenced heavily by the ending. These feelings will often influence how they reflect on the film as a whole, as well as whether or not they will tell their friends to see it. This may seem self-evident to some, but I find the power of the ending is often neglected in the postproduction process. By the time a filmmaker in a low-budget film gets to the end of the film in the postproduction process, he or she is often exhausted and without money and doesn't pay attention to the most critical part of the film.

The Importance of Beginnings and Endings in Your Edit

Flirting with Disaster

After we finished shooting *Flirting with Disaster,* we held a test screening. People responded well, but not as well as we were expecting. Something wasn't quite working the way we wanted, but it was difficult to isolate what the issue was. We huddled and discussed how we could make the film better.

Beginnings and endings are always the first place to go when deconstructing your film to uncover why an audience isn't responding. Upon reviewing the comments and rewatching the film on a big screen, we began to feel we could find a better way to open the film. *Flirting with Disaster* had a unique screwball-comedy style, something that perhaps the audience wasn't being prepped for in the current cut, so it was our job to properly "set the table" for them and establish the tone of the film early on.

We threw around some thoughts and came up with an idea. Our plan involved casting specific types of actors for an opening montage and shooting them on the streets of New York in front of Carnegie Hall. Some would be average looking, some fat, some thin, some beautiful, some strange. Ben Stiller would then add a voice-over to the montage, speaking humorously but poignantly about his place in the world, and reflecting on being an adopted son. David O. Russell then seamlessly edited the sequence together, thus creating a new, strong opening to the film.

The result was startlingly effective, and took the opening in an entirely new direction. We had properly set the table, which allowed the film to truly come together; by making the opening funny and heartfelt while simultaneously laying out the major themes and plot of the film, we had prepared the audience for the odd, wild, and wonderful comic sensibility that would come to define the film and its subsequent success.

So if you see *Flirting with Disaster,* remember that the original opening was not in the original script, nor in the original shoot, but was rather a creative innovation in postproduction that only came about by carefully evaluating the feedback from our early screenings.

One Fall

When we screened *One Fall* for the first time in front of a public audience, we knew it was a very rough cut, but we wanted to get feedback as soon as possible to make it better. The film was a fable about a supernatural ex-convict with a hidden past. As the film progresses, more and more secrets from his past are revealed. Most of the responses were positive, but there was still clearly something that wasn't clicking. The responses were helpful but discouragingly vague. We combed them repeatedly in search of some kind of consensus about what wasn't working with the film.

Marlen and I knew the film needed a strong point of view straight out of the gate, and we were concerned we hadn't got there yet. One of the actors at the screening said he really liked the film, particularly as it reminded him almost of a modern-day fable. Then it hit us—*that was it.*

His use of "almost" made us realize that, while we had wanted the film to play like a fable, something wasn't quite working to fully get that idea across. When we started asking other viewers if they thought the film was a fable, we discovered just about all of them did not yet see it that way.

Once we understood this problem, we went about thinking of new ways to open the film and "set the table," so as to convey our goal of a fable-like atmosphere.

It had also become evident from questioning viewers after screenings that the ending, although good, was not coming together as well as we would have liked. We had hoped that the audience would have had a stronger reaction to the penultimate scene, when the protagonist approaches his dying father in the hospital and tries to save him. But we were very limited with the footage we shot, and the scene just didn't have the emotional kick it needed.

So here's what we did.

We knew that in order to give the film the feeling of a more upbeat, mystical fable, we had to make the opening seem light and magical.

We decided the most effective way to communicate that kind of emotion was to begin the film by leaving the real world behind—briefly—by blending animation with live action.

Now you may be thinking, how is it possible to afford an animated opening and title sequence on a low-budget film, particularly after the principal photography has already been completed? Fortunately, we had two specific assets—Marlen's learned expertise in design and special effects, and our ability to put together a very cost-effective and talented special-effects team through Craigslist ads.

Here's how it played out. . . .

The original opening began in a dark, mysterious location, focusing on the back of the intimidating form of a security guard, whose gait had an ominous limp. The security guard made his way through the hallways of a morgue until he stumbled upon the protagonist, who was mysteriously holding on to a dead female in one of the morgue rooms. Not exactly the upbeat, magical tone we were going for, so we went back to the drawing board and scrapped the entire morgue sequence.

Marlen and I came up with a different way into the film, creating an opening animation—a kind of "mini-plot" sequence with an upbeat song, suggesting the more playful air of an elevated reality.

The solution here lies less in the narrative particulars of our new opening and more on the distinct tone we aspired to set. We really wanted to inspire a particular *feeling* in the audience; in other words, to set the table for them in a very particular way. Using animation in such a playful and novel way communicated to audiences that this wasn't your everyday low-budget film. Overall, with the work the special-effects and animation team assembled, we were able to give our film a very strong opening.

Then we tackled the ending.

As I said, a big part of the film's emotional pull was creating a narrative burn—one that ultimately revealed a mysterious truth about the protagonist. The reveal was an integral part of the protagonist's development and final resolution. The problem was that we felt the final few scenes didn't get the audience where they needed to go, that there was a lack of fulfillment at the film's conclusion.

So we set about fixing it. With our small budget and limited footage for the concluding scene, my sons, Tyler and Forrest, went back through the entire film to pull footage and then built an entirely new ending sequence: a montage of the film's pivotal scenes that illustrated what the protagonist needed to experience internally in order to access his supernatural abilities. This montage then led seamlessly into the climax of the film.

With the new montage, the final scenes now propelled the movie in a different direction—amplifying the major themes of trust and letting go of the past; visualizing the obstacles that the protagonist faced; and tying our theme and the plot together in an extremely emotional and aesthetically pleasing way by showing how the protagonist overcame those obstacles with the help and kindness of others. And the new musical score created for the scene worked wonders for the pacing and timing of the film's ending.

Even with limited resources, we still managed to use the postproduction period to shift the final emotional takeaway, allowing the film to resonate in a way it couldn't before. We had proven Samuel Goldwyn Jr. right. The feeling an audience takes away from the final scenes very often colors the way they feel about your entire movie.

As a further testament to this principle, Hollywood is replete with stories where very specific changes to the endings of big-budget movies ultimately changed how audiences perceived the whole film.

Fatal Attraction

It's one of the most successful and iconic films of its time, but it very nearly wasn't. In the original ending, the female lead (played by Glenn Close) commits suicide, making it look like the male lead (Michael Douglas) had murdered her. Soon after, he is arrested. Douglas's wife in the film (Anne Archer) then finds a tape Close has sent him that may clear his name. The film ends on an uncertain note with what Archer's character will decide to do; we're left unsure whether her husband's marital transgressions will sway her against helping to exonerate him.

When they tested this ending for audiences, the film tanked. People didn't respond well to the ambiguity of the ending. So what did the film's producers do?

They changed the ending entirely. Going back and shooting for another three weeks, they came up with the now-famous final sequence: Close is shot by Archer, making Close the victim and Archer the protector of her family. The filmmakers realized they couldn't make Douglas into the film's hero, as his character cheated on his wife—which is why he was framed for the murder by Close in the original ending. The dynamics here are actually instructive of how audiences respond to filmed stories. They wanted a hero. They needed a hero. But who was left? By recasting Archer's character in a heroic light, the filmmakers resolved this issue. The film garnered six Academy Award nominations, and went on to become the second-highest-grossing film of 1987.

The Hangover

If you happen to leave *The Hangover* before the closing credits, you will experience a very different film. Before the end credits roll, it is never revealed what really happened on that fateful night the guys in the film can't remember. This is interesting, as the mystery of that night is the plot motor that drives the entire film.

But everyone who stayed through the credits got to see a hilarious montage of stills that pieced together the events of the boys' big night. Having still pictures tell that hidden part of the story—even over the end credits—changes everything about how audiences remember the film. It gives viewers a resolution, and solves the film's many mysteries without banging audiences over the head with exposition. Clearly someone in preproduction and postproduction was very well aware of what they were doing, and one could argue that this simple, inexpensive coda to the film ultimately added millions of dollars to *The Hangover*'s gross income.

Casablanca

The ending to *Casablanca* is one of the most iconic moments in all of film history. The final version of the film shows Renault (Claude Rains) delivering the famous line, "Round up the usual suspects." Renault then suggests to Rick (Humphrey Bogart) that they join the Free French Forces at Brazzaville as they walk away together into the fog, commenting on "the beginning of a beautiful friendship."

But this was not supposed to be the final scene. There were specific plans for one additional scene, showing Bogart and Rains sailing with a detachment of Free French soldiers on a ship, headed to the Allies' invasion of North Africa.

When it became too difficult to get Claude Rains for the shoot, however, the plans for the scene were scrapped. Can you imagine *Casablanca* ending with Bogart and Rains dressed up as soldiers on a boat sailing out to war?

And on the other hand, sometimes what you don't show the audience is as important as what you end up putting in your final cut. And yes (pardon the pun), editing always cuts both ways.

Jerry Pickman

When I first met Jerry Pickman a few years back, he was a "youthful" ninety years old. He was a marketing and promotional expert who had worked in marketing from the 1940s through the 1980s. Maybe you've heard of the films Jerry helped make hits: *Psycho, To Catch a Thief, Rear Window,* Cecil B. DeMille's *The Ten Commandments, The Greatest Show on Earth,* and *Samson and Delilah.*

Jerry was one of those guys with a mind so active he simply couldn't stop working: In Jerry's case, the work became producing and creating films. He was still developing projects until the day he passed away at age ninety-five.

During the time I knew him, he would regale me with the most amazing stories of the golden years of Hollywood—a time when everyone he worked with had some kind of world-class nickname like "Slip," "Swifty," "Joey Pots & Pans," etc. Talking to him was like taking a tour through a studio lot in the 1940s.

One of my favorite Jerry Pickman stories:

In the late 1950s, Jerry was helping out at United Artists, a studio and distribution company, and he was privy to this remarkable story: A prominent director screened the final cut of his "picture" (to Jerry, there were no films or movies, there were only "pictures") to the marketing and distribution department of United Artists, which was responsible for distributing the film. It was a unique and unusual comedy, and one the director was very excited about. United Artists viewed the film. They did not laugh. They did not even chuckle. They hated it. As a matter of fact, their collective decision was ultimately not to release the film. Not only did they think the picture was not funny, but in addition, due to the movie's subject matter, they were sure it would receive a "C," "condemned" by the Motion Picture Production Code at that time, meaning it would be seen by no one.

The director couldn't believe it. Keep in mind, this was a time before there were any ancillary markets of any kind. If your film was not formally distributed, you might as well have used it as campfire kindling for all the good it would do you.

Thinking on his feet, the director asked for a week to make some new edits. The decision makers at United Artists were dubious, but decided to allow him a bit more time.

The moment they exited the screening room, the director pulled aside his editor and said, "I am not going to re-edit even one frame of the film. It's great the way it is." He asked the editor to do two things for next week's screening: first, to ensure younger marketing and distribution employees showed up, and secondly to announce beforehand that the film was a comedy, and that laughter was encouraged. Apparently no one had clarified this the first time around.

The second screening was a huge success. Once people knew it was a comedy, they essentially had been given permission to laugh; it was like someone had suddenly turned on the lights. The director was right. The movie worked beautifully. He hadn't changed a single frame, and the brass at United Artists reversed their decision. They would release the film. And then, in a move that would go miles towards abolishing the onerous Production Code at that time (the late 1950s), they recommended that it be released without the approval of the Production Code. And the film turned out to be a major success.

The director?
Billy Wilder.
The film?
Some Like It Hot. Voted the number one comedy of all time by the American Film Institute.

If there hadn't been that second screening, no one would ever have seen or heard of *Some Like It Hot*. Yes, indeed, *sometimes the best edit is no edit at all*.

The editorial process is awesome and powerful, but it's most effective when used with discretion. Just because you have a hammer, it doesn't mean everything you see is a nail. In this instance, Billy Wilder heard such off-the-mark comments from his audience that he knew it wasn't a matter of his film being flawed, but rather of the preconceived notions of those viewing it. It's a lesson in always understanding your own aesthetic in tandem with the views of your audience.

The Postproduction Arena

Music

When you create your rough cut, you will likely use famous music with your picture, as a placeholder for the type of music you would eventually like to incorporate into those scenes, music that, due to your limited budget, you may need to replace as you refine your film. Be prepared—when that moment comes, chances are you might initially feel very disappointed with the replacement results. It stands to reason; music conveys a great deal of the emotion in any story told on film, and you have used very successful and expensive music as your music temp track. Change the music and you change the emotional texture, giving the entire narrative different high points, different low points, and a different emotional rhythm. Granted, there may be instances where you are so in love with your new score that this will not happen, but that is rare.

There are times where it may make sense to approach the owner of the well-known music or musical score you have used in your temp track and ask for a license. The odds are pretty slim that you will get those rights, but if you have a strong personal narrative vis-à-vis your film, it's possible you will succeed. It has happened many more times than I could have guessed in my own career.

One reason is that many musicians are starting to go back into the studio and rerecord their famous songs of years ago. Record companies traditionally own original master tapes of compositions, and often charge prohibitive rates for licensing any original recording. But note that any musician who has rerecorded any of his or her famous tracks (something many of them have done, given how inexpensive it can be nowadays) may be able to license a new recording for you at a much more reasonable rate.

But if you cannot get those original songs, you will be surprised how often your replacement music ends up working well in your film.

Continuity

We all become close to our films. During the filmmaking process, the work becomes a part of you and your life. It's important, though, not to let intimacy with your material cloud your thinking about things like film story continuity.

I have had endless arguments and discussions with filmmakers I have worked with over whether to cut or keep in scenes and specific shots that may have noticeable continuity issues—

scenes where what you see on screen doesn't quite match what comes directly before or after them. Either a prop is out of place, the sun is in a different position, or there's a stray hair on an actor that's only in one shot of an otherwise continuous scene.

Let the storytelling needs of the film inform your choice. Obviously, always strive for the best continuity for your film; at the risk of sounding blasphemous, however, it can possibly work out at times to simply bypass some continuity issues. There are little continuity mistakes in almost every film—it's an inevitable reality when shooting out of sequence, and when cutting together some continuous action from a set of discrete parts. In pretty much every case where we left in sequences with continuity issues, no one in the audience seemed to care, and the film was much better off for not having cut material just for tiny errors.

Scenes Left In

In a film I once made, the lead actor arrived on set one day with a dark suntan he hadn't had the day before. The problem was, in the chronologically prior and subsequent scenes, he had no suntan at all.

It was a pretty obvious discontinuity, but our actor gave a great performance, suntan and all. We left it in, knowing that it did not exactly square with the scenes before and after it. The film went on to do very well, and no one has ever commented about that discrepancy.

Also, actual film equipment, and even crew members, are often left in scenes. In *Harry Potter and the Chamber of Secrets,* when Harry and Draco are fighting (around the one-hour, eight-minute mark in the film), you can clearly see on the left of your screen, among all the young wizards, a forty-something cameraman. But I guess the film survived and did well, regardless of the error. Loving a film goes a long way to either ignoring or accepting its flaws.

Scenes Not Left In

Once, towards the end of one of my films, we had an important (and terrifically acted) scene between two male leads; however, it turned out we had a continuity issue—in one moment one of the actors was on the other's left side, and in the next cut he was on the right. It was a very quick cut, the scene played very powerfully, and it really helped pace the film as it moved towards its ending. In screenings, the scene consistently scored as a favorite, and no one noticed the glitch in continuity.

But the director was unsatisfied with this lack of continuity, so he searched the footage for a take with no errors. He found one, but the performances in the take came nowhere near the power of what we had already screened, continuity problems and all.

I could not convince him otherwise, so we ended up going with the new take. While the new take restored the scene's continuity, in my opinion it lost a lot of its emotional resonance. In addition, subsequent screenings showed a downward shift in positive responses to the film's ending.

You will find you have similar leeway in your special-effects work. When working with a lower budget, there are going to be times where you simply run out of time or money. This even happens in big-budget films sometimes; occasionally, a film's special effects need to be rushed, leaving a good deal to the viewer's imagination.

But here too as with continuity, audiences can be very forgiving. If your film is "working"—the action is flowing and the performances are solid—minor continuity problems and less-than-stellar special effects will not ruin your viewers' experience. When you measure the downside of a few effects that didn't turn out perfectly versus the upside of the majority of your special effects working and adding value to your film, there is no contest—go for the imperfection (when you have a moment, go back and look at the special effects of *Star Wars*).

The broader lesson here is that, while you should always aim high and maintain the utmost expectations for every element of your film, you should never let minor missteps derail your process or shake your confidence. If your story and characters are strong, you and your film will survive.

Color Correction, Audio Mixing, and Deliverables

Your film doesn't end once you have "locked" the picture (i.e., concluded your editing). Color correction, audio mixing, and creating deliverables for your distributor are essential elements of your film. These last technical aspects of postproduction may not seem fun, but they are vital, as they shape your final product and determine how the world will eventually see your film. Having the right colors and a good audio mix can do wonders for the tone and mood of your film; polishing the sound and visuals like this can literally create your film anew—it's that important.

Since these steps are so late in the process and aren't viewed as a "sexy" part of the filmmaking process, they are often overlooked. This makes them all the more crucial in ensuring your movie stands out among the rest. I have seen countless films that are shot beautifully, but have such garbled audio no one can understand what the characters are saying; likewise, I have seen color balance so embarrassingly bad, it takes viewers entirely out of the reality of the film. To see filmmakers go so far only to trip up on these all-important finishing touches always bewilders me.

If the technical side of all this scares you, don't panic. Simply make sure you work with someone with strong postproduction expertise in these particular areas. But there's good news here too (recall Building Block Two); equipment and software have become so economical and user-friendly that these skills can be mastered by many adept people, and can be done in a reasonable fashion without breaking the bank.

Although it may cost more money, it is essential to view your film in a large screening room once your audio mix and color correction are each completed. This is the only way to ensure you know what your final product sounds and looks like on the big screen, and if you'll need to make any additional tweaks before the final version.

Postproduction Rundown: The Last Time You Will Touch Your Film

Study the opening and closing scenes of your favorite films and see how they were done successfully. If you can figure out an inexpensive way to use graphics and/or special effects in these pivotal parts of your movie, it would be a great asset for your project. But don't let the tail wag the dog—focus on your story first, and always make sure to amplify and develop your themes and characters at the beginning and ending of every film you make.

Good pacing and timing are indispensable elements of your film. Don't resist tweaking parts of your film if it seems to move too slowly, too erratically, or too fast. You can shift around scenes, cut scenes, or if necessary add scenes with a smart reshoot or with additional shooting. You may also be able to lessen the impact of bad scenes by cutting back and forth to secondary plot points, "hiding" any scenes that might be weaker than others.

The best edits are those that go unnoticed. A client of mine once referred to one of my postproduction workers as the "Joe DiMaggio" of editing. DiMaggio, the 1950s New York Yankees Hall of Fame baseball player, was incredibly gifted and seamless in his craft. He made everything about the game of baseball seem so easy, so much so that people were not aware of the extent of his amazing prowess on the field. This too is the definition of a great editor and filmmaker.

If you do your research, hire the right people, listen to outside opinions, follow the creative, business, and marketing principles set out in this book, very good things can and will be realized in the postproduction process. And when this time comes—when you know there is nothing more you can do for your film—you will be both excited and content . . . but only for a short time.

Now you have to focus on selling your film. Seems overwhelming, something you didn't sign up for. But don't worry: Pay attention to the next few chapters, and it will all make sense, and will become one of the most exciting and rewarding things you do for your film.

PACKAGING YOUR FILM

Let the Games Begin!

When we finished making The Atlantis Conspiracy, *a television movie I directed for the German television conglomerate ZDF, we turned towards the American market for potential distribution.*

Although it was financed as a television movie, for the American market we decided to package and present the project as an American independent film. We created the appropriate marketing materials— poster, synopsis, stills, everything to position the film in the most favorable light possible. Our campaign complete, we submitted it to the Sundance Film Festival.

Despite our efforts, we did not get in. I got a very nice call from one of the heads of the festival, and he told me that even though the film had a strong concept and was well made, it had just missed acceptance at the festival.

We found ourselves at a crossroads. We could wait for another film festival to come around, but it wouldn't be nearly as prestigious. Our chances of finding theatrical distribution had been greatly diminished.

So we decided to try a different tactic: We revamped the marketing package, reconceived my "narrative" about the film, and set out to sell it not as a feature-length narrative, but as a pay cable television movie.

And it worked. We sold the film to HBO, where it went on to have a successful run on cable, in the home-video market, on television, and on international home video; it even won a few awards along the way. As a matter of fact, though the film is many years old, I still receive foreign residual checks for The Atlantis Conspiracy.

Same film, different approach and packaging . . . and quite a different result. To convert a potential failure into a success through packaging demonstrates just how vital that element can be to the success of your film and how important this kind of strategic thinking can be.

You have completed your film, but your film's life is just beginning. The good news is you are now about to enter an entirely new stage of the process—if you package and promote your film correctly, you'll be just a heartbeat away from jump-starting your career.

In much the same way you crafted a personal narrative to aid in financing and mounting your film, it is now more crucial than ever that you create a marketing narrative for your film. Begin with the work you've already done crafting your particular narrative, expanding it based on whom you wish to sell to. Your primary goals with your first film production, your "calling card" (that is, how you will be introduced into the industry), should be simultaneously twofold: First, you wish to capture the attention of any future industry employers and financiers, as well as production entities, agents, and managers. Second, where your current film is concerned, you must set all your sights on securing a distributor or sales agent looking for a strong, marketable product.

Keep in mind, the process of selling your film and building your career doesn't end with one rejection or just one film. We live in the age of *American Idol*, where everyone believes they get their one spin at the roulette wheel, and if their number doesn't come up, their one shot at glory is gone. That makes for great drama on a reality TV show, but that's not the way things work in the film and television industry.

In fact, I argue just the opposite: In the film and television industry, you can now have as many "bites at the apple" as you wish. If your film or project doesn't work, simply try another, and then another. The director, Rian Johnson (*Looper*), shot many, many short films before he was able to find enough success to persuade investors to invest in his first narrative feature. There is no endgame here; the true goal is to keep working, creating, and producing. Ben Lewin, the director of *The Sessions,* was a major success story at Sundance in 2012 when his film was picked up by Fox Searchlight for distribution. It was his first American feature. His age when the film screened at the festival? Sixty-six.

And then there's the story of Fred Stobaugh. He spent his life working as a driver, and when he was ninety-six, his wife of seventy-three years, Lorraine, passed away. He had never written a song before, but he was so heartbroken that he wrote a tune for her called "Oh Sweet Lorraine." He then submitted it to an online music contest, and the song ended up being produced as a single and made it onto Billboard's Hot 100 (breaking a record for the oldest songwriter). And it was in the top ten songs purchased on iTunes and has also become a hit overseas. Based upon this success, he has just written another one that will be produced soon. Not bad for a ninety-six-year-old ex-driver.

While there's no limit to how many shots you get, there are certain common missteps you can easily avoid. The old mainstay of the independent-film marketing narrative is a fixation on forever highlighting how inexpensive it was to make your movie. Kevin Smith, for example, made it widely known that *Clerks* was produced for only $28,000, as did Robert Rodriguez with *El Mariachi*, made for under $10,000.

This model has played itself out. In fact, it's exactly the opposite of what you'll want to focus on. Do not brag about how inexpensive it was to make your movie. Film distributors understand this dynamic. *The Sessions*, starring John Hawkes, Helen Hunt, William H. Macy, and many other name actors, enjoyed a strong theatrical release by Fox Searchlight, including a blitz of television commercials and newspaper ads pitting the film head-to-head with *Les Misérables, Lincoln,* and *Argo.* And, as those movies did, *The Sessions* garnered nominations at both the Golden Globes and the Oscars. And do you know the budget of the film?

One million dollars.

You want to know why you didn't know the budget? Because Fox Searchlight didn't want you to know. They didn't want the film to be stigmatized as "just another low-budget indie film"; it has become so easy to shoot a low-budget feature these days that the market has become flooded with competition. And what's worse: Most of them are painful to watch. The default narrative of the proudly "low-budget" film has earned a negative connotation, and more often than not audiences will assume your film, like many out there, is just plain bad. If Fox Searchlight didn't want to hurt their film this way, why would you want to do this to your film?

If you've followed the advice in this book, your film will be better than most of what's out there. So your packaging narrative shouldn't be about equipment, cost, and expedience, but rather all about your story, your unique aesthetic, and all the tailored marketing strategies you and your team have crafted using Building Blocks One and Two. And now it is on to the Third and final Building Block—marketing and distribution through social media.

Preparing the Sell

How do you go about packaging your film in the era of new media? Your "sell" must comprise all of the following elements, whether your goal is to impress an audience, a prospective industry financier, or a distributor.

The Press Kit

Your film's press kit should use your narrative as its launching point, building outward and expanding where necessary. The press kit brings it all together: It is the bible for your film's marketing plan, outlining all the strengths of both your film and you as a filmmaker. Your original "pre-film" narrative may have changed since preproduction, and now that you have completed your film, you will be able to see how it matched the perceptions, theories, and feelings you highlighted in the beginning. Did it turn out the way you envisioned? Did your actors, script, and/or postproduction work take shape the way you originally thought? If you focus on what surprised or inspired you about the production process, you can amplify and modify those elements in your narrative to propel your film further. Perhaps you can highlight a breakout performance of an unknown actor, or tout the outstanding ensemble work you have assembled. Use the strengths of your finished piece to add new angles to how you package your film, enriching the story behind your film and making it all the more compelling.

Look to the Internet for examples of press kits and take note of how they're written and put together: How do they nail the overall feeling and sound they're trying to project? You might even consider hiring someone from a freelance writing site, or from a university (an English, journalism, or marketing major, perhaps) to do the writing for you in exchange for credit.

The Poster

The goal of a poster is to stand out from the crowd. Use interesting colors, use a little space, or all the space—if you were walking down the street, would it draw your attention?

Making a poster is not as difficult as it sounds. Here again, new inexpensive technology comes into play. Photoshop makes poster design easy, and you can always go online or to a nearby art school to find artistic and technical talent to assist you. But be careful in your artist choices because many people can design, but not just anybody can produce good design.

And who knows your film better than you? Bring samples of your ideas to people you respect. Do what real marketing companies do: Brainstorm ten or more concepts to choose from; there's no rule limiting yourself to just one approach. Use IMDbPro to browse some great posters. (There are many good posters on trailers.apple.com.) Most star-driven posters will put the lead actors front and center, but chances are that you will have no major stars in your film. However, don't worry—there are plenty of terrific, innovative posters produced every year. You just need a little bit of emotional creativity. Notice how the best ones instantly evoke a feeling or inspire curiosity about the film.

When we were creating our poster for *One Fall*, a film about a mystical search to find oneself, our poster for the theatrical release showed the protagonist in a subtle blue backdrop at the very edge of a cliff, peering down into a deep valley encompassing a town, evoking very specific emotions of curiosity, mystery, and danger.

But when we went to the home-media market, where the market is more direct (you're competing against a multitude of other DVD and Blu-ray covers adjacent to yours in stores and kiosks and on websites), the poster changed to one of our scenes where the protagonist was seemingly "walking on water," against a backdrop of new, much bolder orange and gold colors. We also placed parts of a prominent review from the *New York Times* citing the mystical aspects of the film on the Blu-ray cover. Different market, different poster.

The Trailer

Despite the abundance of firms existing solely to create advertising for movies, you can create your own great trailer in-house with the assistance of your editor. We once had a major ad agency offer to help us create the trailer for *One Fall*. We evaluated their plans and creative direction, and ultimately decided their approach wasn't right for the film. We wanted a trailer that better captured the essence of the film, encompassing both the magical reality and the elevated realism that we thought were the movie's greatest strengths.

My sons, Forrest and Tyler, came up with an idea, executed it, edited it, and presented it to the film's distributor. It was exactly what a trailer should be: good pacing, building in energy and emotion, teasing the narrative beats of the film without revealing too much, all the while alerting viewers of the big, moving moments waiting for them if they were to come see the movie.

In addition, music in a trailer is very important. Today, many successful trailers are less about telling you what the film is about and more about creating a "music video" of sorts to give you the gist of the movie.

Everyone loved our trailer, and it even went on to win a major award given to outstanding film trailers. After it was seen in theaters, and subsequently on YouTube, it proved to be a major selling device for *One Fall,* sustaining so much public interest that hundreds of thousands of people would go on to view the film on Netflix after our theatrical run.

Even shorts can have compelling trailers. That might sound a little crazy at first—a trailer for a short film? But why not? Since your short is short, your trailer, too, should be shorter than the trailer for a full-length film. Even if your trailer is thirty seconds, it can still demonstrate your storytelling prowess, as well as your editorial craft. It is much harder to tell a story in a condensed period of time—especially in only thirty seconds! Show that you have the skill to do this, and you will have a great opportunity to quickly and easily entice and captivate new audiences.

The Marketing Report

Creating a marketing report is hard work, but it can turn into a major asset in your film's arsenal. The marketing report is a document that outlines your film, analyzes your market, and details a strategy of how to connect with that market.

For example, a colleague of mine made a faith-based film,

analyzed who the market for his film would be, and then came up with a very savvy marketing plan to get to that market: He contacted the top five hundred churches he thought would like his film and offered a free, one-night-only premiere simulcast (by Blu-ray on a large screen), while also sending film-related marketing materials to these churches. In return for this free premiere, the churches agreed to sell his film on Blu-ray (with Blu-ray bonuses) that night after the screening, and then for several future weeks at their churches. His strategy worked exceedingly well, with many of his viewers liking the film and event so much that they bought it on Blu-ray directly after seeing the film's premiere, and the word of mouth helped continue Blu-ray sales for many weeks thereafter. And this was in addition to his traditional marketing efforts.

Even if you don't end up using your marketing report, creating one shows your thorough understanding of your film and its avenues for potential success. It may also open up your ultimate distributor to new ideas about your film not thought of previously.

Remember, your first production is like an interview for a career in filmmaking, so it is not just your movie that will be put under scrutiny. The industry will be looking closely at you, and the more chances you give yourself to shine, the better your odds of connecting with the viewers and making contacts you'll need to really kick-start your career. Demonstrating you know your way around the business side of the movie business with a marketing report helps you make an impression as a thoughtful, knowledgeable filmmaker.

Need help getting started on your marketing report? Go online to look for samples and for examples of marketing and advertising, and never be afraid to turn to the English and journalism departments of nearby universities for students to assist you.

Although your marketing report can be as creative as you want it to be, it needs to be grounded in hard-core research. You have to do some digging to discover the precise kinds of people who will best respond to your film—and why this is so. You need to know where these viewers are, as well as the best ways to approach them. Is your film an urban story geared best to a big-city audience? Or will it find more appeal in the Bible Belt? Knowledge of your desired audience, as well as what about your film entices them most, must always be on your mind.

Jerry Pickman once described to me a great example of creative marketing. He was working with Alfred Hitchcock to come up with the marketing strategy for his new film, *Psycho*.

It was during one of these meetings that they came up with an inventive idea that broke with the conventions of how movies were screened back in the early 1960s: They insisted there be a policy preventing anyone from entering the theater once the picture started. Back then, the same picture would run back-to-back without any breaks, with very few (if any) trailers, and no commercials in between any of the screenings. Thus, it was fairly commonplace for people to come and go at various times during the screening of a film.

So Pickman and Hitchcock's plan was big news. Jerry told me there was both the "official," publicity-stated reason for the strategy, as well as Hitchcock's own personal reason behind it. The official rationale went this way: Since a major film star was killed in the beginning of the picture (spoiler: Janet Leigh as Marion Crane is famously murdered in the shower in the first act of *Psycho*), they felt the audience would be upset if they paid money to see a star and came late, only to find out that she was dead, *and* that they missed the crucial scene.

But Jerry told me Hitchcock had a different reason for wanting to make sure the audience saw the lead die early in the film.

He felt if people came in and saw a leading actress killed in the beginning of a movie, it would really make a strong aesthetic statement: Doing away with Janet Leigh early in the film would blindside the audience, knocking them back on their heels. Hitchcock thought this choice was so unexpected and so powerful that seeing the film from the beginning was the only way audiences would be able to experience the film emotionally. Subconsciously, they'd reason that if a film could kill off Janet Leigh right at the start, who knows what else could happen?

Theater owners initially resisted Hitchcock's strategy, as they felt such a stringent policy would result in fewer people seeing the film. But once they saw how effective this counterintuitive measure was, they all fell in line and supported the legendary director's decision. Ultimately, Hitchcock's restrictions led to increased viewership for *Psycho*.

This theory was repeated with great success by Harvey and Bob Weinstein more than fifty years later, when they killed off star Drew Barrymore very early in their movie *Scream*. This is a rare example of an excellent strategy that blends aesthetics and marketing, creating an ideal fusion of "show and business" that captivates viewers while making an artistic statement at the same time. If I read an idea even close to being this innovative, in a marketing report, I, as a producer, would be extremely impressed with the filmmaker's creativity and talent.

So you see how important a marketing plan—even a theoretical one—can be in the overall package you must create for your film. And in today's marketplace it is essential to also develop a social-media marketing strategy (Building Block Three) as part of the marketing plan in your final package that you will present to the outside world.

Social media is exploding, and a carefully planned strategy using this asset can become your greatest ally. For example, in my previously cited faith-based film example, the filmmaker initially found the appropriate five hundred lead churches by mounting a very aggressive and pinpoint social-media research effort. He then followed it up with a strong and continuous blogging campaign as he began cajoling those churches into premiering his film. More specifics on social-media marketing when actually releasing your film are found in chapter 10.

Resist the Urge to "Broadcast" Your Film to Everyone

Filmmakers

I know it's hard, particularly when you see all the social media that is available at your fingertips, but you have to resist your urge to broadcast to the world that your film is finished. Do not start a Facebook page, Twitter account, or a film website, and do not update IMDbPro, screaming to the industry that you have completed your film. The same goes for any social media designed to promote your film via your trailer (this means no YouTube or Vimeo). Do not post anything that says your film is done—*not yet*, that is.

Instead, you should highlight your intent to spearhead these social-media initiatives (Building Block Three) in your marketing report. I would even suggest you attach hypothetical samples of how you will promote via the Internet. But again, I reemphasize this: Do not go public just yet! Having your film announced and exposed this early on can only lengthen the time the industry can monitor it before you make a sale to a distributor. As discussed in previous chapters, you may end up stigmatizing your film as a nonstarter—something that's been kicking around for months with no bites—even though you haven't even actively begun trying to sell it. Loading up social-media platforms with information about your movie so early on accomplishes nothing in the marketplace for your career; it just strokes your ego, something you should save for when you do eventually get your film distributed to audiences.

Remember, once you start your social-media campaign, you're effectively presenting your film to the outside world; in so doing, you lose an enormous amount of control of its marketing direction, and the longer it sits out there without a distributor, the worse it will look for your film's narrative. To work this hard and to make the mistake of a premature social media release would be tragic.

Be patient; it will be time soon enough to announce your film to the world (in this case, after you read chapter 10).

Actors

Actors, in addition to creating your marketing package for your first film as a filmmaker and actor, by following the steps in this book you are simultaneously in the position of having a marketing package for yourself as a working actor. If you have followed my previous suggestions, you now have created:

- your personal "trailer" (in this case, your reel);
- a combined narrative/marketing report describing who you are and how you would sell yourself as an actor (this can be much shorter than needed for a feature film);
- a poster (for actors, the poster artwork can include a flattering production still of you); and
- a regular headshot (not "Barbie-dolled" up in Photoshop), focusing on the strengths you highlighted in your narrative/marketing report; or

perhaps a series of small narrative headshots that tell a story. For example, Jeremy Davies's headshot was three pictures of him standing in the woods looking in different directions. And taken a step further, Luke Wilson never had a headshot; his "headshot" was the movie he was in, *Bottle Rocket*, which helped develop his career.

So you now have a great selling device for your acting skills. However, the same restraints on social-media marketing for filmmakers hold true for you—perhaps even more so—when you're putting together your marketing package. Do not put anything on Vimeo, YouTube, or any other online forum (unless it's private and password-protected). Why? Remember chapter 4 for actors? Because that's exactly what every other struggling actor in the world does. Your odds of standing out from the millions of other people who announce themselves online would be—just to give you a rough, back-of-the-envelope estimate—about nil.

I am not saying never to go online, but to go online at the right time. And we will cover when precisely to do this in the following chapter.

Do research. Target people you think would find appeal in your skill and in your personal narrative. Attempt to contact them through e-mail, call their assistants, talk to friends of friends. Pursue any leads that you may have. Once that contact is made, you offer to send them a DVD or private link to your acting reel. By being so direct, you can let potential employers and casting directors know you're dedicated and how important their project might be to you. Be sure to follow up a few days later.

And don't get discouraged. If you send out a hundred DVDs or e-mails with access to your private link, perhaps none will hit. Simply send out a hundred more, or if it is too costly, then focus on sending out your private link. If you've built a body of good work, eventually you'll get a nibble. The more people you contact, the better your chances become.

An additional benefit to doing it this way is that casting directors, agents, managers, and people in the entertainment industry will now be impressed that you have completed your film. Some of them may have actually worked with you in securing some of the roles in your film. They will be nicer to you because you are a filmmaker now, and perhaps one day they will need you or you will need them to book one of their clients for a role in one of your films.

The Final Frontier

Creating your package is the last creative piece of the filmmaking process. Never, ever underestimate the value you can add to your movie by wrapping it in a professional, well-researched, and well-targeted package.

Your goal is to make it difficult for someone to say no to you. Because, more often than not, the industry's first instinct will be to turn you down categorically, even before they see your film. The challenge is turning that "no" into a "yes." And the more tools you give a potential distributor (or employer, as the case may be) to sell you, your film, and your talent, the easier that challenge becomes.

Always remember: You know more about your film than anyone else. No one else has the intimate knowledge necessary to be more passionate, honest, and creative about *your* film than you do—so show them that!

Packaging your film is an exciting and arduous task, and you'll need to flex a different sort of creative muscle than you're used to. But don't worry, because you've already created a base from which to work. Your drive will come from you and the personal narrative you've been honing throughout the entire filmmaking process.

As you gain experience packaging your first film, it will become second nature to you—a new and wholly essential part of your skill as a filmmaker. And guess what? When you go on to sell your next project, you will quickly find out that you already have all the tools, know-how, and experience to become the marketing expert for all your future creative work and ideas.

You now have the package. It's time to introduce yourself to the world.

DISTRIBUTING AND MARKETING YOUR FILM

Hey, Look at Me!

Film festivals tend to bring out your highest expectations. You've worked hard on your movie, you've got confidence in your work, and your friends have told you you're talented and that your film is great. So you start to believe the hype. At least a little. Believe me, it's easy for even the most spartan filmmakers to get swept up in all the festivities and enter expecting to be crowned the next King of Hollywood—particularly with a first feature film.

So it was with my first trip to Sundance. We were there to sell the first film I produced, Spanking the Monkey. I thought the film had a real shot. It was funny. It was edgy. It was different. I felt sure it was going to be big.

This was 1994, before Sundance had become the cream of the independent film world—and the most important marketplace for its distributors. One could argue that this particular year was kind of when Sun-

dance really became the "Sundance" we know today. A few high-profile acquisitions at the festival that year really caught the industry's attention, proving this wasn't some breeding ground for purely uncommerical art-house cinema.

But of course, in the days leading up to the festival, we had no idea this year would be any different than the last. What's more, I had never sold a film before.

An example of how things were changing at Sundance was David O. Russell and my decision to not show up for Spanking the Monkey's *initial screening. Each film chosen for the competition section is screened four times during the ten-day festival. We were told, which was true up until that time, that distributors did not start bidding for new films until the second half of the festival, so there was no rush to get there. Nowadays the bidding can get so furious that just the opposite is true, so it becomes imperative to be there the very first day your film screens.*

So we skipped the first screening. This, we would soon see, would become a major mistake on our part.

One of the favors we had worked extremely hard to get during production was the use of a 35-millimeter camera, equipment very uncommon for an ultralow-budget independent film in 1994.

It was so rare that when Spanking the Monkey *had its first screening at Sundance, the film projectionist completely botched the screening. Not knowing about our 35-millimeter coup, he simply assumed it had been shot on 16-millimeter (as most independent films were in those days). So the projectionist did not put on the right aspect ratio for our film.*

We weren't there, but we were told that this made

everything look strange—nothing was framed how we framed it. Viewers could suddenly see things, such as boom mics, equipment, and other props on the screen, that were meant to be cropped out. And nothing marks a film as a rinky-dink operation faster than seeing a visible boom microphone in a scene. The first reviews completely called us out for it, saying (among others things) that poor us, we didn't even know how to position a camera.

Not the most auspicious start for a film. So we got no interest from the distributors. Our film was dead in the water.

"Well," I thought, "my career in the film industry was certainly short-lived, and I hope that dentist in Jamaica, Queens, is missing me right now as much as I'm missing him."

But just before returning to my "cement-shoe" work, I came up with a potential solution.

We had Cara White, a great publicist, working with us, and we really believed we had a strong film on our hands, so we just had to figure a way out of this bad break. Recall that at Sundance, if you've entered your film in the main competition section, you are permitted to screen it four times over the festival period. This is one of the things that is so good about Sundance, and it's one of the reasons the festival has done so well over the years; it gives you a chance to fix your marketing mistakes, allowing you an opportunity to build a plan around your film as the days go on, and after each successive screening. You effectively have "four bites at the apple," which is wonderful, and a particular lifesaver if you need a mulligan as badly as we did.

Cara and I found a foreign-sales agent who was in-

terested in licensing our film. It wasn't much, but it gave us a backup plan in case all else failed. We then went to see a reporter from Variety, who was there to write daily updates from the festival.

Rather than dwell on the negativity of our first review, we continued to spin a strong narrative, informing the reporter we had some roused-up interest for distribution after only one screening—which was entirely accurate. He then reported this information in that day's Daily Variety, giving us all the daylight we needed. Cara and I hit the streets, tracking down any distributors we could find and letting them know that, despite the major technical glitch in our first screening, we had still managed to generate some real interest in the film. Keep in mind: This was long before the advent of Twitter tweets and Facebook posts and status updates for communicating. All communication was still analogue—otherwise known as using our feet to walk around and actually talk to people (I know, what an odd concept).

We had three more screenings to build upon the new and constantly evolving narrative that we were now a film with distribution interest, a film that, when screened in the proper 35-millimeter aspect ratio, was getting a great audience response.

With this ammunition in hand, I reapproached the distributors who went to the failed first screening and those who, based upon the initial bad review, were not interested in going to the screening at all. About 50 percent of them came to the third and fourth screenings, and by that time the buzz on the film was heightened; add to this an extremely strong audience response, and *by the end of the fourth screening, distributors were approaching me wanting to distribute the film.*

We met with a few distributors, and by the start of the awards ceremony on the last day of the festival, we had chosen Fine Line Features, the distributor we felt was best suited for our film. I actually signed the deal with Fine Line on a piece of paper supplied by a Sundance volunteer in the back of the Sundance awards-ceremony room, minutes before the Sundance awards program began (one in which we won the Audience Award for Spanking the Monkey).

It worked: I sold the film, and we were on our way.

Good collaborators, a strong marketing package, and a smart, always-up-to-date narrative literally saved my career.

Knowing Whom to Target and Making Your Sale

Being a filmmaker will never just be about making films; you will always have to know your market. Creative freedom on the part of artists is best when informed by knowledge of what people want—and what they will want to buy.

Read the industry trades. You'll discover the way studios and major production and sales entities are optioning shorts and documentaries from anyone, to develop into feature films, television shows, web series, and all of the emerging digital platforms. More than ever the opportunities are there.

Knowing your target viewers, as well as *why* you're targeting them, is crucial to any filmmaker's first project. Often it breaks down this way: A short film is great for exposure (which can lead to career-starting opportunities), while feature films should be aimed more at gaining exposure *and* making sales to distributors.

For the sake of clarity, let's divide the target audience of your first film into two categories.

The Public

You have your film and your package (your "calling cards"); your job now is to hit the streets to find viewers for your product.

Where should you look? Everywhere. Once again, you are only limited by your imagination. As you now know, some of my opportunities emanated from secretaries of next-door neighbors and fiancés of filmmakers, in such exotic places as a steam room in Queens, etc., so don't close any doors. Remember: Your big break could come from anywhere, and the more you put you (and your film) out there, the more chances you have to stumble across an opportunity that could launch your career.

Film Festivals

Film festivals can be an excellent (but by no means the only) way to surround yourself with potential financiers and employers, as well as with possible ways to distribute your narrative feature and short film. And, yes, some film festivals retain industry clout—Sundance, Toronto, South by Southwest, Cannes, and certain others. They will always be worth the effort.

Eddie Burns told *Entertainment Weekly* how his first feature film, *The Brothers McMullen,* had more than 150 rejections. His film career seemed to be dead in the water, when one day, while he was working as a gofer at *Entertainment Tonight,* he chased down guest Robert Redford and gave him a copy of his film as Redford was in the elevator leaving the show. A few weeks later he found out that his film was accepted to Sundance, where it went on to win the Grand Prize, and became a very successful film that launched his career.

But often many lower echelon tiered festivals are, at best, an inoffensive way to drop some money and screen your film; at worst, they can be a serious time suck and (sad as it is to say) a great way to get exploited.

These festival organizers (much like screenplay contest organizers) know that filmmakers are eager for exposure and recognition. They know this eagerness can be leveraged against filmmakers who are hungry for any accolade they can attach to their film—even if it's from a festival that will never register the tiniest blip on the industry's radar. If you look candidly at most of the hundreds of film festivals in existence, it becomes obvious that some of them are more moneymaking machines for the festivals themselves than they are ways for young filmmakers to realistically jump-start their careers.

Much like the too-early social-media blitz, "festival dancing," as it's sometimes called, is often more of an ego boost for a filmmaker than it is a savvy career decision—and carries with it the same perils. If I check someone's background on IMDb-Pro and find their films attached to only lower echelon festivals, my first read will be that the film isn't very good, and that the filmmaker's ego is probably more important than the work.

You should note that this doesn't necessarily apply to short films. As there's much less of a market for such projects, I am more forgiving when I see a short that's been featured in a number of different festivals. In a market not particularly receptive to short filmmaking, these festivals can be a good place to go, particularly to leverage that short and forge contacts and meet peers in the industry.

In addition, placing your short in a specifically themed festival, like a comedy festival, a Jewish film festival, or a gay film festival, for example, can turn out to be beneficial for your film.

Remember my story about *The Atlantis Conspiracy*? Once I saw that it had failed to get into Sundance, I did not simply bounce from festival to festival, hoping to win a random "audience award" or "critics' choice" ribbon. I reinvented my marketing pitch and sold it to HBO as a successful movie.

Sales Agents, Distributors/End Users, and Self-Distribution

How do you find outlets for potential sales? Building Block One: There are no shortage of stones to turn to see what people are watching, and where they're watching it. It's always helpful to see what Netflix is buying, or what Hulu is buying, and to use IMDbPro and other industry sites to see who's making deals, and which entities are working with films you like. There are also many websites and blogs that can be helpful (for example, Mediakitchen.com and lightsfilmschool.com).

And once you target the right entities for your film, the way for you to approach distributors and sales agents ties back into the marketing plan you created as you developed your idea, your film, and your film's package.

The beauty of shopping your film nowadays is the ease with which you can show it to anyone, anywhere. No longer are you bound by location or screening equipment, a freedom that gives you unlimited opportunities to sell you and your film.

Domestic Sales Agents

A sales agent is an entity who assists you in attempting to secure a licensing agreement for your film for theatrical distributors, broadcast televison, cable, DVD, and the entire digital universe (for example, video on demand and online TV), and many more outlets. They are not your personal agent/representative (which we will discuss in the next chapter), but specifically, the agent for your film or project.

Go to the Internet, check recent films that got into film festivals that you like, and note who represented them. Google articles about sales agents, find the films they represent, and check their websites. Research as much as you can.

I am an advocate for working with sales agents when necessary. But when you are first starting out, it can be difficult to get a good one to work with you. As we've already discussed, given how easy it is to make a low-budget film in the twenty-first century, the market is constantly overflowing with competing projects. The chances of getting a powerful sales agent to represent your film may seem slim, but use what you've already learned to reach out to someone who can help your career—no matter how untouchable they may seem. Even if he or she cannot formally represent it, they may still watch and become a fan of your work, which can lead to another important career contact down the road—someone you can call again in the future for advice and career development. And the really strong and decent agents (there are more of those out there than you think) will often come up with a recommendation for someone else who might be a good fit for your film.

Another tactic is to ask the cast and crew from your film if they know and can recommend any great sales agents who could either rep or help your film. Many times an actor's agent may have a colleague sales agent at his or her firm who will take a look at your project. If agents or managers have a client in your project, they want it to succeed as much as you do, so they'd be willing to help.

And there are many strong up-and-coming sales agents. You don't always have to get the top domestic sales agents. Don't be put off by lack of experience if everything else checks out well. Examine their track records and references very carefully. And be wary if a substantial "consulting fee" is required up front.

Foreign-Sales Agents

A foreign-sales agent will be in charge of licensing your film for foreign territories. They will also more likely want to sell your film if it has had some sort of distribution in the United States. A good place to start your search for a foreign-sales agent would be on IMDbPro. Check out the films these agents (or companies) have represented in the past. You'll want to be meticulous when researching candidates for this position, as this person will be representing both you and your work. Peruse their websites to get a sense of who they are.

You can contact these agents by e-mail and then follow up by phone. Many foreign-sales agents are located in the United States and are easy to contact. In addition, major film and television sales conferences occur quite a few times a year in the United States. Read the industry trades to find out on what dates these events happen, see what markets your targeted sales agents and companies attend, and check out their references. Scope out the films they're actively selling; if they are films you like, then make appointments to meet these agents at the sales conferences. There are also associations that monitor sales agencies, so look to see if any complaints have been lodged against any of the companies or individuals you're looking to make a deal with.

As you can readily see, your success with everything in this chapter, from attending important festivals to finding a good firm to sell your film overseas, will boil down to finding the right team to market, promote, and sell your film's best, most salable qualities. You already know the drill for successful hiring—just follow the principles I laid out in chapter 6. As with any other position, set up reasonable milestones for the team to achieve, all based on the parameters already proposed to you in the strategic sales plans you will have discussed before agreeing to be a client.

When hiring foreign-sales agents, it's a good idea to get projections from them as to how many territories they think they'll be able to license, and how much money they envision getting per sale. Use those numbers as goals, and have your continuing sales relationship be contingent upon their performance. In other words, if they reach certain economic goals or dollar figures within a certain time period, agree to re-contract to continue selling your film for another year or two. If they do not meet those goals, specify that the rights to sell the film revert back to you. You should get a lawyer to work out the terms. If you set up your agreement this way, then everyone has a dog in this race. If they have a problem with this, then I would be concerned they are not confident in the numbers given in their initial projections.

Distributors/End Users

If you cannot find a sales agent, you can approach a distributor or end user directly. There is a distinction between the two (the end user is the actual venue you want to be in; the distributor is the one who approaches these end users to get them to exhibit your film), but for the sake of simplicity, we can put the two entities together. Your initial goal is to make personal contact with the distributor/end user, give them your marketing package, and try to arrange a screening of your film for them. Although you might think that making the contact with a distributor/end user is a very difficult task, you will be very surprised about how approachable many distributors are. Remember, they are in the business of finding product, and with your strong narrative and marketing approach, many more doors will open for you. Here too the Internet and independent film organizations are your best friends.

Once you attract a distributor/end user, there's a bit of a dance you've got to do with them. Often, particularly for first-time filmmakers, they won't want to take the time to attend a formal screening, but would want to see it online. I don't recommend this, as you always want to control who sees your work and ensure that they see it in the best possible forum at this critical juncture. But you may not have a choice. If you do have to send them your film online, please make sure that it has a temporary encoded number that is password-protected, so that you have some sort of security for your product.

Traditionally, end users, particularly in foreign markets and ancillary markets (e.g., cable, Blu-ray, and digital), are difficult to approach directly. Often these are pretty big, fairly unwieldy companies that aren't very good at changing the script of their decision-making system, and an unknown independent filmmaker approaching them in order to sell a film will rarely be met with much attention.

Nevertheless, there are those rare instances where a filmmaker has had a previous connection with these end users or simply gets lucky—so never say never.

When I went out to sell *Spanking the Monkey* overseas, I was introduced by phone to a gentleman named Klaus

Volkenborn—a well-known, successful German filmmaker who had connections to ZDF, one of the largest distributors and end users in Europe—in the hope he could help me make a direct sale. Although we didn't end up selling *Spanking the Monkey* to ZDF, it began a conversation between Klaus and me. He told me he was always interested in getting into the American film market.

Remember Klaus Volkenborn? Over the next decade, he would become one of my closest friends and collaborators, as well as a financier for many of my films by approaching foreign distributors and end users. It was a great partnership—and friendship—until sadly he died unexpectedly a few years back, after setting the record (as he would often remind me, with a wink) for being the longest surviving person in Germany with one kidney—and a transplanted one at that.

In addition, nowadays there are so many new end-user platforms being developed, particularly in the digital and online space, that these outlets have become much more receptive to directly licensing independent films than they have been in the past. And I see this pattern only continuing to grow.

For example, I can predict that one of the biggest companies in the world (a non-mass-media company, with a net worth of approximately $110 billion) will become one of the largest producers and licensors of films and television shows in the world, and their primary reason for reaching this goal will have nothing to do with the films and shows themselves!

Who am I talking about?

Does the name "Amazon" ring a bell?

Amazon will spend millions of dollars on creating television programming exclusively for viewing by Amazon Prime members (for an annual fee of $79, customers get free two-day shipping on millions of items, as well as digital access to their library of television shows, e-books, and movies). And most remarkably, in a case where the cart is now leading the horse, Amazon's goal in producing television product is to attract people to get a Prime membership so that they'll be more likely to purchase Amazon's *other* products—books, clothing, appliances, etc. A report from Morningstar, an investment-research firm, shows that Prime members purchase more frequently than nonmembers, spend twice as much annually, and tend to buy more expensive products.

This is just one example; more will be coming down the road soon.

If you have an interest from a distributor or end user, realize that the parameters of the deal for a first-time filmmaker can be somewhat standard; they can be found by doing some research online or by working with that inexpensive (particularly since you now have a deal) lawyer.

Self-Distribution

Self-distribution means cutting out the middleman and going straight to the theaters (and eventually to subsidiary markets such as digital, DVD, Blu-ray, television, and foreign) to have them exhibit your film. This is a very interesting possibility—it gives you more control but requires more time, work, and money on your part as you take your film around the country from theater to theater.

And even if you decide not to self-distribute, it is important to understand how film distribution works, because it teaches you what a distribution company does every step.

If you can strike the right deal with the theater owner and forge the right distribution plan for your film, it becomes instantly possible to get what every filmmaker needs for their product: exposure, reviews, and eyeballs in theaters all over the country. The economics of self-distribution doesn't end in the theater either. The exposure of a theatrical distribution is almost like a hard asset for your movie for licensing to additional theaters and to your ancillary markets. If your film does well financially and/or gets good reviews (did you know that the New York Times has a policy that it will review *all* films that play in a theater in New York City?), then more theaters and ancillary buyers will see that your film has juice behind it, thus allowing you to expand your theatrical release and eventually charge higher licensing fees, and further helping you establish your career as a creative and financial success.

If you follow the tenets in this book, you will already have many of the elements needed to self-distribute:

1. Press kit (check)
2. Marketing strategy (check)
3. Trailer (check)
4. Poster (check)
5. Package (quasi-check): Some of the work you've done on your overall package will help you develop a release strategy. Having a specific release strategy, detailing precisely how you are going to release your film, knowing whether you should focus on big or smaller cities, and deciding which of these regions you should have your premiere in are crucial in any plan to self-distribute. You've done plenty of the research to answer some of these questions already. So just finesse it to fit your theatrical-release strategy.

Here are some additional elements that you may need to consider for self-release.

Theater Bookers versus Theater Owners

While a good theater booker can be a great asset, helping you pick the right venues for your film and coordinate with theater owners to maximize publicity, I am not 100 percent convinced you need to employ someone to fill this position. Many self-releasing filmmakers have regaled me with stories of theaters so eager for product, it takes nothing but a phone call to get them interested enough to negotiate a deal. Deal terms and interests will vary with different theaters, and you might hear the term "four walling" (where you buy out the whole theater), or "back-end split," where you negotiate a percentage for you and a percentage for the theater owner of your film's income from that theater. The more you bring to the table with your package (which should include a great poster, advertising, a great trailer, a strong marketing strategy, and well-curated reviews), the stronger your negotiating position. As with all strategies, be straightforward and as transparent as you can; let the owner see everything in your distribution plan, and make them a partner in your efforts to get as many people to see the film as possible. Test the market first: See, if possible, what the theater looks like, or if not possible, check it online. Also, call the theater owners directly and find out what arrangements you could make with them, and then decide if you want to attempt to approach them yourself or use a theater booker.

Marketing Companies

These are companies or individuals that place advertisements for your film in cities where the film appears. Here too you should do some comparison shopping by interviewing a few marketing companies, to see what the costs are, and consider if you can't simply do it yourself inexpensively. Often marketing entities will say they can get a better price when booking advertisements, but this is not always the case. Ask potential marketing companies what their pricing on such ad-buys would be, and then directly call the same end suppliers to compare prices. Think about where the ad itself will come from. Will it simply be a tweaked version of the poster? Are you talking about online ads? Newspapers? TV? Radio? Will the marketing entities come up with a strategy of where the ads should be placed for maximum effectiveness? You may be able to do the entire job for less, but at the end of the day you may determine it might not be worth the time and trouble, in which case hire a formal marketing partner.

Publicist

This is a tricky position. A publicist, the person who creates publicity for your actors, film, and you, can be a very important addition to your team *depending on your film's particular needs*. Cara White was exemplary for us at Sundance in assisting to sell *Spanking the Monkey*. However, if you are not at Sundance and are self-releasing, you will find yourself with an entirely different set of publicity needs. Remember: A primary goal of a publicist is to initially get you exposure in the cities your film opens up in. Newsprint, online, local TV—anything. And giving your publicist a strong marketing strategy that you have already created will get him or her excited and add a new dimension to your film. But if you're unknown and self-releasing, and if your film is small—without big stars, without a built-in marketing hook—even the best publicist may not be effective.

Keep in mind, too, that publicists are often great salespeople, and can sometimes promise the moon. Always check around before you make any decisions; if you find one you like, discuss realistic strategies, set goals, and most important, see if you are compatible and feel comfortable with the level of promises you've been made.

Social-Media Marketing

On the face of it, social-media marketing can seem like a major asset to an aspiring filmmaker. And it can be. Handled correctly, it can be a thoughtful, inexpensive, and well-targeted way to get great exposure for your project. This type of marketing, highlighted in Building Block Three (The New Social-Media Environment), can be very successful, but involves constant vigilance and work.

We are in the midst of a social-media revolution. As Frank Rose stated in *The Art of Immersion*, if the three leading broadcast networks had broadcast nonstop for the last sixty years, that would equal 1.5 million hours of programming, which would equal less than what YouTube has uploaded in *only six months' time . . . in 2010*. And according to YouTube's latest statistics, users are now uploading 1.5 million hours of programming in less than ten days' time!

Or put another way, according to Cisco Systems, in 2005 the Internet carried thirty billion gigabytes of video, e-mail, web transactions, and business-to-business analytics. And in 2012 that number increased by more than twenty times, including two trillion minutes of video alone every month, which translates into more than a million years per week of video appearing on the web.

To make your ideas catch on, word of mouth is essential to reach your audience (resulting in about 20 to 50 percent of all purchasing decisions), as Jonah Berger points out in *Contagious: Why Things Catch On*. But at present only approximately 7 percent of all word of mouth occurs online. And regarding YouTube itself, 50 percent of all videos on YouTube have less than five hundred views, and only one-third of 1 percent of all videos have more than one million views on YouTube.

So how do you create a buzz in the social-media universe?

Here too there are no hard and fast rules for success, but you can maximize your opportunities for success, whether you release your film by yourself or assist your distributor in releasing it.

You need to start with a base of operations for your social-media campaign, which nowadays can start on sites like Facebook, Twitter, MySpace, YouTube, Google, and Pinterest (to name a few). As you know, I'm not a big fan of websites, so I lean towards creating a Facebook page for your initial work, because it is easier to set up and it's easier to interact with your prospective viewers. Granted, building a website may ultimately work better for your needs, but starting with a Facebook page while you build your website would be a good way to go.

Once you have your Facebook page or website, make sure you set it up with the marketing materials you have created. Studies have shown that the best way to achieve online marketing success is to create *empathy* for you and your project. Knowing this, start using social-networking searches to find audiences who will be interested in your film. And not just film sites. Just the opposite—if you have a film that is about basketball, start by going to basketball sites; if it's about travel, go to travel sites; fashion, fashion sites. That is where you will find your most loyal audience base, who could kick-start a word-of-mouth buzz for your film. For example, with *One Fall,* a film about spirituality and healing, we started approaching yoga and spiritual institutes across the country.

Also, because you are marketing a visual product, blend your online written materials with video and photo-sharing networking sites in which you share your trailer or exciting parts of your film. Which sites? I can list some sites now for you, but things are changing so rapidly that my advice is to google social-media sites immediately after you read the book, and the most contemporary social-media-site floodgates will open for you.

Once you are "in action," it becomes imperative that you maintain your activity, whether it be tweeting on a regular basis, updating your materials, subscribing to more social-media sites, posting, asking questions, starting discussions, sharing, etc. You should also ask your viewers to do something (e.g., visit your Facebook page or website or "like" your Facebook page). However, now that everybody is asking to be "liked" or "followed," it can get annoying. Often it is more effective to thank people for liking, following you, or supporting you; that goodwill goes a long way to expanding your following. Your goal is to constantly engage your audience with your story.

And regardless of how successful you may be in your initial attempts, by creating a social-media marketing campaign, you are simultaneously gaining very important skills, experience, and a base for operations that will continue to grow and to serve you better and better as you develop your film career. Kevin Smith is a prime example of a filmmaker who has astutely cultivated his online presence over the years to his maximum benefit (more than 2.5 million followers on Twitter).

Another example of the effectiveness of social media is the success of the film *Paranormal Activity*. *Paranormal Activity* is one of the most successful low-budget horror movies of all time. Shot in a week for a little more than $10,000, it's become an iconic part of the horror vernacular and has spawned four sequels. Here is a case where the social-media strategy turned out to be just as ingenious (if not more so) as the film itself.

The movie began with a limited release in targeted college towns—an ideal audience for horror. Then they encouraged people to "tweet their screams"—effectively gaining thousands of positive mini-reviews. This unprecedented type of re-sponse caused the film—as well as the media coverage—to go viral. This combined well with the team's shrewd and uncon-ventional advertising campaign, which actually incorporated the audience reactions as much as it did clips of the movie itself. Seeing real audience members squirm with fright got every-one's attention.

Moreover, on the film's website, they had a "Demand it!" button that led the user to a website where they could vote for the film to come to their city. It was likely a pure publicity stunt, but it gave the movie a cultlike following. And democratizing the decision to give the film a wider release went a long way towards establishing a devoted fan base on which to build the franchise.

Many have since tried to replicate the success of *Paranormal Activity*—mostly without the same kind of results. Remember: Social-media marketing is very much terra incognita. It's in its infancy. And because the nature of social-media platforms is evolving so quickly, what works today will probably be out-dated tomorrow.

But one thing will always be true. A well-thought-out online strategy has to be blended with other forms of traditional mar-keting. Human-to-human word of mouth will always be a major goal for marketing your film. CinemaScore is a film ser-vice that highlights this fact. Every Friday, CinemaScore asks people coming out of about five theaters at a film's first screen-ings to grade ("A+" to "F") the movie they just saw. And with these word-of-mouth scores CinemaScore then determines the potential success of the movie. And CinemaScore's predictive successes have been uncanny, much more so than positive critic reviews. A list of some of their "A+" scores, while all not criti-cal darlings (*The Help, The Blind Side, The King's Speech, The Avengers, Titanic, Argo,* and *Tangled*), ended up being very successful films. And new companies like Rentrak, which polls twenty theaters across the country, are popping up as able competitors.

So as inclined as you may be to see social media as a panacea for your marketing concerns, you must find ways to blend it with direct, traditional marketing.

Nevertheless, the Internet has provided a true carnival of marketing options. Targeting groups online, blogging, guest blogging, Twitter, Facebook, advertiser support online and in general, targeted, web-based sneak preview screenings—they are all just the tip of the iceberg. And as time goes on I marvel at the inventiveness of filmmakers as they soberly and thoughtfully devise brilliant new ways to market their films through social media.

A word of caution here—because social media is growing so fast, we are in the midst of a filtering process that will continue for quite some time, and will determine which digital services are reliable and which are not.

As often as you hear of great online stories, you hear of problematic online stories. A few years back my work on a film I did was dishonestly criticized online, a critique that was factually incorrect. But I was lucky. I got in touch with the website and provided them with my support evidence, and they took down that incorrect and misleading posting. Others may not be so lucky, so try to be as cautious as possible, and be quick to try to remedy any problems that appear online.

As excited as I am about Building Blocks One and Two, the story about Building Block Three is only just being written as we speak, and, when it reaches maturity, it could eventually eclipse Building Blocks One and Two in its potential to change industry patterns.

Your Film's Deliverable Materials

You will need proper deliverable materials for your film (i.e., all the proper movie formats for your film's theatrical projecting equipment) to give to any theater owners that show your movie. Different theaters will have different requirements, so please make sure you are clear as to what they need from you, be it 35-millimeter prints, DCP, Blu-ray, satellite uplink material, or some other format.

This would be a good time to draw on the reservoir of good-will you've built up with your crew. If, for example, you hired a line producer with postproduction experience or an editor, you can now call him or her for some advice as to how you can create the release materials the theater owner needs. You are theatrically releasing your film, so your crew should be very ex-cited about those prospects and willing to help. Theaters will also be very helpful in these areas, so don't be afraid to ask each of them what they'll need.

Just as with your initial screenings, it is also beneficial to test ahead of time how the film looks and sounds in the the-ater in question. Here too I have found theaters very willing to help. You have to remember: This is one of those times in the filmmaking process where everyone you'll be dealing with will share the same goal—you and your exhibitor both want your film to be a theatrical success.

Your Film's Release Strategies

As you read these distribution strategies, perhaps it's occurred to you to fuse and combine some of them. As it turns out, many distributors are doing exactly that. A release strategy that's gained a great deal of traction is a same-day (or a few weeks later, or even a few weeks before) digital release in conjunction with initial theatrical release. Many are finding this can be a cost-efficient way to gain viewers in a marketplace of diverse media venues. Digital releases are great for maximizing sales, while theatrical releases can gain you valuable exposure, allowing you to increase what you charge for ancillary market licenses when more distributors and end users become interested in showing your film.

You can even approach distributors and offer to make a "split rights" deal with them; this means your team will handle all matters pertaining to theatrical release, while the distributor takes care of selling to ancillary markets. And if you decide to release the film simultaneously, or near simultaneously, into the digital market, be up front with your plan so you can coordinate your overall strategy. In this way, you control your theatrical release and keep costs low, while another entity sells ancillary digital rights. If you have a strong theatrical-distribution strategy, your project can start to look very appealing, proving very effective for both parties.

Selling, licensing, and distributing your film—getting it seen, in other words—is one of the most nerve-wracking and exciting things you'll do as a filmmaker. Because the nature of distribution changes so quickly, opportunities to make money and get your film seen will always arise. And whether you're immediately successful, or whether your sales grow steadily over time, your first film is only the first step in the process to building an entire career in the entertainment industry.

So things are looking very promising right now.

By the way, how's your next film coming along?

YOUR NEXT FILM

The Career Maker
(and How Failure Can Breed Success)

There will be none of my film escapades leading off this chapter.

You now know how to make a short or narrative feature, how to prepare the marketing and distribution materials, and the best ways to introduce the world to your product. The Three Building Blocks of today's film and TV industry (Internet, new-media technology, and marketing and distribution with social media) are no longer a secret to you. Now you have all the tools you need to break into the film and television business; you're ready.

Making your first film is really all about making your next film; it's the first step towards building a career, and ensuring you don't remain a one-hit (or no-hit) wonder.

When do you start this second film? You started it the moment you began your first. I am not suggesting you make two films simultaneously; rather, think back to that list of ideas you came up with when we went through the development and script-writing chapters. That list should have been rich with creative possibilities. Your second favorite idea—start developing that one! Do it in your downtime, while waiting for your actors to be available for a shoot, while waiting for the first editorial cut from your editor, while developing the marketing materials, or while developing your list of possible distributors and end users. Remember the theories of creativity and inspiration, and always be looking for ways to exercise your creative muscles. If you get too bogged down in your current film and feel like it's too much to direct your creative efforts elsewhere, put whatever ideas you're developing aside for now. Let these ideas sit. They'll be there when you have time to come up for air, along with a new perspective from your time away from your original project.

But you do have to start it. And sooner rather than later. Why?

Because this book is all about empowerment. There is almost nothing more frustrating, no feeling more powerless, than finally finishing your film—a creative venture that has dominated your time as you rethought and rewrote and recut and reworked—and then sending it out to the world only to find you can do nothing but wait. And wait. *And wait,* all the while anticipating responses from your end viewers.

By starting on your next film, you put yourself back in control of your life and your career. That sense of confidence is a great thing to have! It also presents a strong picture of you to the industry at large: one that shows you are relentless, hardworking, already working on your next film and that, no matter what, you will stop at nothing to be successful.

The striving and hard work never ends. After we did *Spanking the Monkey,* we thought it would be easy making the next film. After all, *Spanking the Monkey* won the Audience Award at Sundance, was one of the best reviewed films of the year, and did well theatrically when it was eventually released by Fine Line Features.

The next one should have been a layup. A two-and-half-foot putt on the eighteenth green. An empty net goal.

Not even close.

While *Spanking the Monkey* was still hot, we submitted David O. Russell's next script to the industry at large; more than twenty-five entities were given the treatment. And the response?

(Yes, that is silence you are reading.)

We succeeded in getting only one lukewarm low-ball response from Fine Line (who had distributed *Spanking the Monkey*), and that was it. Most felt the script was too dark, or the comedy too odd.

I was convinced that if we had a live person, an audience to "pitch" the script to, we could make that person see it in an entirely different light—for all its brilliant potential—and want to produce the movie. And I knew who that very person was: Trea Hoving, a very talented and astute distributor at Miramax. If you ask Harvey Weinstein, he would tell you she was the "soul" of Miramax—and that her taste and skill at acquiring wonderful films was one of the main reasons Miramax became as successful as it did. This isn't always the case in the industry, but Trea was and is a terrific person as well.

The only problem was that she was in acquisitions, not in production. The lines of demarcation are very sharp and defined in the film industry. Someone in acquisitions does not have any say or influence in which films the company would develop and produce. Meeting with Trea, then, would more than likely be a waste of time, particularly because the production side of Miramax had already passed on the script.

But you already know what I am going to say next: *What did I have to lose?*

Up to that point I had never dealt with Miramax on a production level. Actually, at that point, I had never dealt with anyone at any company anywhere in matters of film production. Despite the fact that I had a successful film under my belt, I was still the guy only one step away from making deals out of a steam room in Queens. But I had heard they were a very flexible, open company, so we took our shot and called Trea, asking her to read the script, as well as to meet afterwards to talk about it.

After a few days, David and I went to her apartment on the Upper East Side of Manhattan. We worked up our "narrative" for the film. We came prepared.

She had read the script and liked it very much. We then went further into the script, even acting out a few scenes to give her a taste of the sensibility of this oddball comedy.

It was a great meeting. She really "got" the film, and although she was not in the production department, she promised to approach Harvey to recommend he make the movie.

The script was *Flirting with Disaster,* which turned out to be a very successful film for all those involved. And Trea Hoving became one of its executive producers.

So just because you've completed your first film, don't stop now! You can't! Even if your first film is a success, you will want to have your second one ready (or in production) immediately; even if your follow-up is not well received, you have to keep on pushing forward—always.

There's plenty of ways to go with your next project and plenty of good it can do for your growing career.

Make a short film. You are learning and will continue to learn while developing your team of collaborators, your aesthetic, and your knowledge of the marketplace. Continue to make them, innovating and refining your style, while you look for feature opportunities. Follow the same principles listed in this book. It can help in the following ways:

- You will now have yet another product to show potential investors as you continue to look for feature-film opportunities.
- Any prominent cast you meet for your short can possibly work with you on your feature.
- Working will further develop your talent.
- If it generates enough interest, you can consider developing your short into a feature-length film or television project.
- It shows that you are in this industry for the long run, and that this was not just a fanciful, one-time hobbyist outing for you.
- It gives you the chance to do something fun and completely in your control, free of most of the market pressures that you'll face down the road.

Develop and make a feature-length film. If your film is turning out really well, there is nothing to stop you from developing and making a feature-length film! Using what you've learned in this book, you have made a low-budget short or feature film that should be highly marketable, with quality production values and possible tax breaks for your investors, and bolstered by a great marketing package. You've put together a great team of collaborators, and you have been very straightforward, honest, and transparent with your investors, letting them know what you are doing all along the way. By this point you have actually completed the film and learned a good deal from it, so as good as this one is, you can be confident the second one will be that much better.

The beauty of developing your second film while working on your first is that you don't have to reinvent the wheel. Everything you have done and everyone you have met on your journey for the first film are contacts and resources for your next film, and for growing your career. You've learned from your mistakes, and although you'll make new ones, you'll always be getting better at your craft. This is one of the few times where indeed you are a hammer, and everyone you meet and everything you do on your first film are nails for your next film.

A Word About Follow-Ups

Be decent to everyone you meet—*particularly* those who have passed on your project, or who were not initially so helpful. This can be advantageous for two reasons:

1. I have found that if you return to those who have passed on your first film, they will become very impressed with your fortitude. Because you've made a film, you've earned legitimacy and people will appreciate your not holding their previous business decisions against them.

2. These distributors and end users are career builders for you. If you are not pleasant when they reject you, chances are they will not want to deal with you in the future. Saying no is an unpleasant action for the distributor and end user as well as for you. If you make

that experience as positive as you can, chances are they will be more open to look at your future work. Just by being cordial, you can turn rejections into contacts and potential allies down the road.

A successful foreign-sales agent is an example of such an ally. The United States is one of the few major countries in the world whose government does not help finance films directly through state-sponsored funding. When you develop relationships with foreign agents, you are also opening the door for possible cofinancing for your future projects.

You may soon discover that most foreign-sales professionals will pass on films without recognizable stars. That's just the nature of the business, and these professionals have a very good grip on what they can sell and what they can't. This makes it all the more important to nurture any and all relationships with this part of the industry. Because when you come back with your second feature film, with some talent attached and an established track record, the odds they'll want to get behind your film will skyrocket. They can now assist you in licensing and potentially even point you towards international cofinancing opportunities. This, if you'll remember, is exactly what happened with Klaus Volkenborn, something that helped jumpstart my entire career.

It's easy to take criticism of your film or a professional rejection very personally. You've invested so much in your work that when people don't respond to it, their reaction stays with you. Don't let it. This is a business. If people can sell your work or make money from your work, they'll want the relationship. This, too, is why it's helpful to keep in touch with those in the promotion, criticism, and marketing industries. These people are not your enemies or friends; their primary goal is to get stories that are noteworthy. So treat them nicely (as they deserve—they are just doing their job, after all), as they can be very beneficial to your future career.

I remember being at an awards dinner and sitting next to John Sayles, the very talented and Academy Award–nominated filmmaker and writer. He had a stack of newspapers on his seat, and he was going through them nonchalantly, separating them into two distinct piles. I asked him what he was doing. He said he was reading the reviews of his latest film, making sure to send thank-you notes to those critics who gave it a favorable write-up. These writers were his true allies, and he was thoughtful enough to recognize that, building contacts along the way for his next films.

Another example of, in this case unknowingly, having "failure" being used for your benefit: One of my clients was asked to rewrite a script for a major film studio. The studio made the announcement in the industry trades. Things were going well for him at first, but in the end, as is often the case, he was replaced by other writers. The project went on for years and years, with many writers joining the project after his departure. With each trade announcement that a new writer had been hired, his name was included as one of the original writers—even though he'd been off the project for years. This led to him getting many new writing assignments, simply because everyone in the industry associated him with that prominent film. Eventually the original film he was hired for came out, but because the story had changed so much over the years his name was no longer included in the credits. He didn't care. Because of his attachment to the original film, and the free promotion he gained throughout, he was able to secure two other films from major studios.

Representation

This section is for you personally, not for your film. Much of what you may still be wondering about will probably involve representation. When is the proper time to seek out a manager or an agent? When are their efforts most needed? At what point in your career can you realistically get one to work with you?

Generally, when you need a representative you can't get one, and when you don't need one, they'll all want to represent you. A strong, committed agent is a great benefit for a seasoned filmmaker to have. The value is not nearly as clear for someone who is at the beginning of a career. So don't worry too much if you find none of them calling you back.

At present, film and television agencies are going through a period of great downsizing. Many of the good agents have become overwhelmed with the sheer quantity of the clients they have taken on to represent. As a new filmmaker, the chance you'll get lost in the crowd is significant. I have heard many, many stories from clients about how happy they are to have prominent representation, yet, at the same time, they complain about how their agents don't ever get back to them. Saying you're represented sounds amazing at cocktail parties. Having your agent never get back to you, however, does nothing for your career.

Although getting an agent may be problematic at times, managers are a different story altogether. Although managers, unlike agents, cannot by law seek out employment for you, they can nonetheless be very helpful to your career. Also, unlike agents, they do not have to be licensed, which means there are many more of them out there, so you must be very careful when researching their reputations.

Do not seek out representation until you have at least one

product to show. The more product you have to show, the better results you'll get from your initial research; you will have a specific canon of work that will enable your agent to immediately identify your skills, aesthetic, and product. This helps for two reasons: (1) Good agents have an instinctive knack for creating their own "narrative" about their clients, encompassing why they're talented, why they're interesting, and why someone should want to work with them. Seeing your work is key to enabling that process. And (2) it also makes it easier for representatives to delineate a clear strategy as to how they can assist you, and what specifically they may have to offer. This will help them channel their own efforts in a way that dovetails with your particular talents.

How do you search out a good manager? Review the hiring section in chapter 6, placing particular emphasis on personal recommendations. In addition, use IMDbPro to find up-and-coming managers interested in growing their client base—the kind who will consider a novice filmmaker, and who (ideally) live in your city. Personal contact is vital to a successful representation agreement. Ask for recommendations from his or her clients, and ask for those not-so-prominent clients to speak to, to get a better sense of how the manager works with everyone on his or her list.

When you find a manager interested in working with you, ask him or her to lay out a strategy as to how they will help further develop your career. Pay close attention to specifics, particularly the kind of contacts they have, and to how these relationships can be helpful to you. Now that prospective representation can view your film—a creative piece of you—it's essential that they "get" you and your work if they're going to help you advance.

If you connect with a manager and want to formalize a

working relationship, have an attorney look over the agreement. Again, set up particular milestones for the manager directly related to the strategy you two originally agreed on. Spell out what you'd like him or her to help you accomplish within the first twelve to eighteen months of the agreement, thereby allowing you to pull the plug in your relationship if these goals are not met.

And whether you work with an agent or manager, the key is that you've created a product. An agent at Creative Artists Agency (CAA) saw a short film a student of mine had made using the steps from my seminar (and the steps now laid out in this book) and said, "This short film shows me that the filmmaker's got chops." He said it showed talent, drive, and best of all, mixed art and commercial appeal. The agent asked what the filmmaker wanted to do next: Does he have an idea for a show? Would he be interested in writing for several new TV shows that the agent was representing? Or does he want to continue making films? As you see, the doors of the film and television industry are both interchangeable and open; it's just a matter of getting to that door with a good product to sell.

Mistaekes, I've Made a Few

As you move forward in your career, do not be afraid to make mistakes. More than likely you will fail . . . often. But if you follow the instructions in this book, you will have the economic opportunity to fail continually until you don't. And then you will find your voice, and then use it . . . over and over again.

And when you succeed on your first film, congratulations, you're on your way! But if you find yourself despairing, please take the following action:

Go to Springfield, Massachusetts, and visit the Basketball Hall of Fame, even if you're not a sports enthusiast. Go to the middle of the second floor. You will see a Michael Jordan exhibit. He is the greatest basketball player ever to play the game. Pay close attention to the words at the exhibit's entrance. They express a sentiment so important they are by design the very first thing you see that is a tribute to one of the greatest athletes of all time:

> *I've missed more than 9,000 shots in my career.*
> *I've lost almost 300 games.*
> *26 times, I've been trusted to take the game winning shot and missed.*
> *I've failed over and over and over again in my life.*
> *And that is why I succeed.*

So there you have it.

CONCLUSION

You Did It!

This is it. We have come to the end (or the beginning, depending on how you look at it), and I hope there will be many, many sequels for you as your career moves forward.

In this book, I have listed many challenges that I have encountered in this industry. And the only constant is that they all worked out. Perhaps they could have worked out in a more ideal way, but they did, with successful execution and end products.

For example, when I graduated school I was armed with a law degree, a master's degree, and a PhD; I thought I was ready to take on the world, and I spent the next two years looking for employment, and I found nothing. Talk about a full-on failure. The reason I took on the "steam room" job of producing a television music series was not because I wanted to, but because I had no alternative; nothing else was going on in my life at that time. And as you know, that project was a full-fledged failure. I saw no silver lining at that time. But looking back at those years, the lessons I learned and the people I met during that time of failure became essential parts of my future successes.

Closing Credits

It starts with the Three Building Blocks, which changed the rules of the game. The advent of new-media markets has demolished all previous models for success, and will continue to do so in the future. The changes in the last few years alone have dwarfed all previous changes by comparison over the last few decades. These changes are fundamental and will have long-lasting effects. My son Forrest likes to call this new-media youth generation, which he is part of, "The iMe Generation™." Multitudes of advances in technology are all, seemingly, for the same purpose: to tell other people (especially ones we don't know well), "Look at me! I'm here, and I'm doing this!" It becomes so overwhelming that often people don't end up listening to one another. Instead, they are just giving their opinions to the world 24/7, using the "like" and "comment" functions so readily accessible on social networking sites, just to feel connected.

With all this in mind, it becomes the task of the new generation of filmmakers to create movies, TV, and other entertainment that can bust through this logjam of social discourse—or lack thereof.

And you will be ready because with this book you now have the tools to turn your inherent creativity into a marketable product that can lead to a long career of making great films and television programs. As you move forward, bear these things in mind:

Good news: It has never been easier to make a film.

Bad news: It has never been easier to make a really bad film.

Good news: New media has opened up many industry vistas for those who now need product, and there are many new ways to gain access into this industry.

Bad news: It is so easy to make a movie that the competition has gotten even greater.

Good news: If you follow the tenets of this book, you will find ways to distinguish yourself from the pack—thinking differently, and at times counterintuitively, really does end up making a positive difference.

You now understand all of the needs of your films, both the "show" and "business" parts of the show-business industry. Use this book as a reference guide. Go back to it often to remind you, to guide you . . . and to inspire you.

And look at my own story. I am a former "steam-room producer" who believed in a script that got him fired from HBO, only to end up with a completed film that had a disastrous first screening and was initially passed on by every distributor that screened it. But look at the end result of all my persistence: success.

And remember, ignore others who try to tear you down. This is your personal race, your personal journey, and the only limit you have is the one you set for yourself.

In the world of entertainment, you will never have regrets about your failures—but you will regret the things you wanted to do but were too afraid to try.

What I'm giving you is simple, hard, and profound—all at

the same time. But here's the bottom line: By reading and following the lessons in this book, you can begin to control your own destiny. It may not happen overnight, and it may even take years, but if you are committed and willing to do the hard work, it will happen.

Remember, in this industry and, more important, in this life, never take the path you're given; always take the path you make—when you do that, you've already succeeded.

ACKNOWLEDGMENTS

I know how collaborative the process of making a film is, but through writing this book, I came to realize how collaborative the process of writing a book is as well. It's been an incredible journey, and I'd like to thank some wonderful people.

First and foremost, I want to thank my wife and collaborator, Marlen Hecht. Without her, this book, from inception to completion, would have never happened. She first came up with the idea of me giving a seminar, "How to Break into the Film and TV Industry." She then suggested that I turn it into a book, and she was there, fastidiously and constantly, every step of the way, with her intelligence, passion, beauty, and insight, to make this book better and better.

The DNA of my sons, Forrest and Tyler, is on every page of this book. With their input, knowledge, inspiration, and drive, they made it better than it could have ever been.

If it wasn't for the creative input, love, and support of all three of my family members, I would probably still be in that steam room in Queens.

My remarkable parents, Ben and Sylvia, were always a shining example of how to live and love in life, and for that I am eternally grateful.

My brother, Marc (and his wonderful wife, Ann), both amazing people, who have always been there for me. And growing up with an older brother who was always caring, smart, patient, and loving, and served as my lifelong role model, is a blessing beyond words.

My sister, Shira, and her family, whose constant loyalty and love knows no bounds.

Rich Greenberg, a dear friend and collaborator, who spent hours with me on the book, always there, always willing to help, with a grace, intelligence, and good cheer that is so rare to find.

Tina and Kurt Hecht, Stanley and Joan Hecht and their family, Manfred Hecht, Stanley Vincent Pullano, Frank Gruber and Matt Greenberg, for their continued love and support.

My friend and book agent, Laura Yorke, has an integrity, passion, and drive that are just remarkable. Her never-ending commitment and excitement for the book are things I can never thank her enough for. Also to Carol Mann and her whole team at the Carol Mann Agency.

Turning my seminar into a book was an incredibly arduous task, something that would never have happened without the keen intelligence, skill, patience, and experience of Henry Ferris and Cole Hager, my remarkably talented editors at William Morrow/HarperCollins. They challenged me to make this the best book possible, and their work made the book better than I thought it could ever be. And thanks to Matthew Patin and Lelia Mander for such a thoughtful and thorough job of copyediting and overseeing the book, Jessie Edwards and Alaina Waggner for helping get the book out there, and to all the other terrific people at William Morrow/HarperCollins.

Klaus Volkenborn, for being one of the best friends and collaborators a person could ask for. He is missed by everyone who knew him or saw any one of his films.

Ingmar Bergman, for sparking my interest in the film world, Bob Dylan and Bruce Springsteen, whose music always lines the back of my mind and spirit.

Bibby and Prince, and all my dogs from growing up in Brooklyn. I mean actual dogs, not dawgs (part of me still wonders if Bibby is walking around the Bronx right now).

Prince Nigel Soladu, for promising me riches beyond my wildest dreams.

Enrico Palazzo, for his beautiful voice and crime-solving prowess (even though he looks a lot like Frank).

Levain Bakery, for being there through my darkest hours, and Tad's Steaks, for the best eleven-dollar steaks in Times Square.

Thanks to everyone in the film and television industry who has made my career possible. Through the good times and the not so good times, the kindness and help that many colleagues have given me over the years has been invaluable and so generous. Again, many thanks.

And most important, to all the past, present, and future filmmakers, this book is for you. There is nothing to stop you now. It is a great industry we're in; now make it even better.

And if you, the hesitant or burgeoning filmmaker, still need more support, you can e-mail me at info@deansilvers.com, and I will try my best to respond to all of your questions.

Good luck.